madMinis

First published in January 2010

British Library Cataloguing in Publication Data
A catalogue record for this book is available from the
British Library

ISBN 978 1 84425 520 7

Library of Congress control no. 2009936760

Published by Haynes Publishing,
Sparkford, Yeovil, Somerset BA22 7JJ, UK
Tel: 01963 442030 Fax: 01963 440001
Int. tel: +44 1963 442030 Int. fax: +44 1963 440001
E-mail: sales@haynes.co.uk
Website: www.haynes.co.uk

Haynes North America Inc.
861 Lawrence Drive, Newbury Park,
California 91320, USA

Designed by Lee Parsons

Printed and bound in the UK

TO CONVERT FROM IMPERIAL MEASUREMENTS TO METRIC

Pounds (lb) to kilograms (kg)	multiply by **0.454**
Pounds-force feet (lb/ft) to Newton metres (Nm)	multiply by **1.356**
Inches (in) to millimetres (mm)	multiply by **25.4**
Feet (ft) to metres (m)	multiply by **0.305**

mad Minis

The crazy world of modified Minis

IainAyre

Contents

Introduction 6

1 Minissan: God Save The Clown 8

2 The Suicide Chop 14

3 Chuck's Fire Engine 20

4 Orange and Juicy 24

5 The Magic Bus 30

6 Turbo Triple Miniac 34

7 The GT40 Mini 38

8 International Rescue 42

9 The Miniha 46

10 Moking 50

11 The Rotary Club 54

12 Offroad 60

13 Street and Strip 64

14 Carmelie 68

15 Trikes 74

16 The Multicultural Mini   78

17 Varnishing Point   84

18 The Roofless Cooper   88

19 The Madmen   92

20 Pooh and the Hunny Pot   96

21 Mad Frank   102

22 Admirable Nelsons   108

23 Z-Cars   114

24 Ice Racing   120

25 Mini Limo   124

26 Mini Marcos   128

27 The Psycho Twini   134

28 Mini Kit Cars   140

29 Mini Mouse   146

30 Posh Minis   152

More Mad Minis   158

Introduction

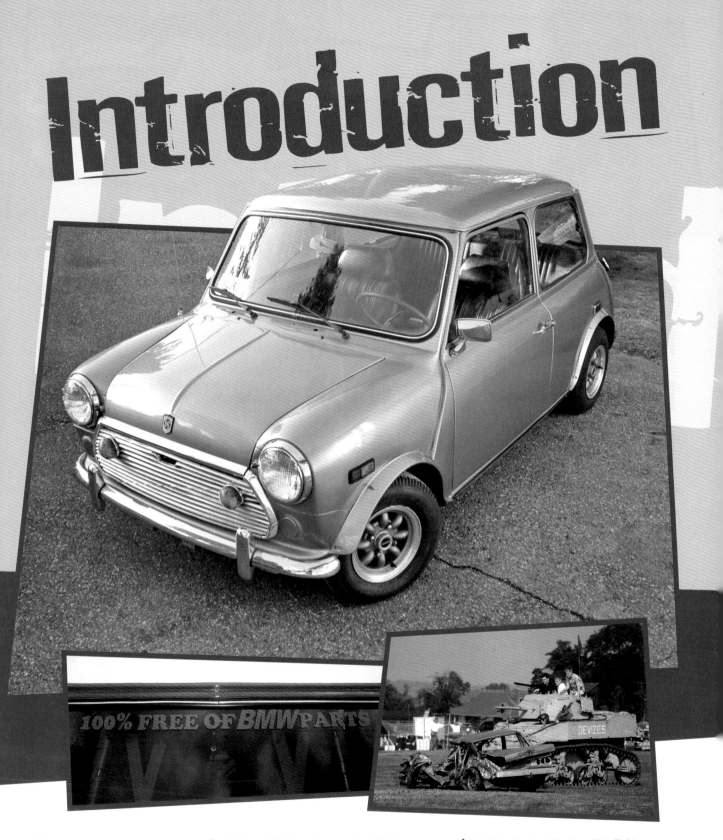

↑↑Bubble is my current Mini. It might finish up as a unique MG Mini. Or a unique MG Turbo Mini. Or a 4x4 Minzuki. Or a stretch limo. Or a Z-Car.

↑'100% free of BMW parts'... many classic Mini enthusiasts really don't like BMW's Mini-inspired pastiche. In a *MiniWorld* survey 50% liked them, 50% hated them. I'll start writing about them as soon as somebody fits one with an interesting engine.

↑The Volvo Crush: the Southern Mini Club know just how much Mini owners used to hate Volvos, driven by smug people who feel safe and don't bother to look where they're going. It's harder to spot Volvos now, as they look like BMWs or Hyundais.

I've been *MiniWorld*'s North American correspondent for a few years now since moving to Canada, but before that I was writing about Minis for a long time in the UK. I started with *Mini Magazine*, and later graduated to the more senior *MiniWorld* magazine.

Some of the Minis featured in this book have been seen in *MiniWorld*, though for their appearance in *Mad Minis* their stories have usually been extended from my original notes, and offer significantly more detail than is possible in a magazine. Also, magazines are edited to be more polite than books, so if I think something's bollocks I can say so here.

A few of the stories have been seen in the Australian magazine *The Mini Experience*, which is also a top read.

The reason I'm still writing about Minis after more than a decade is mostly because of their owners. Mini people are sociable, eccentric, opinionated, cheerful, creative, helpful, and endlessly interested and interesting. They also keep coming up with new and fascinating angles on the Mini theme.

As with most Brits, there are several Minis in my own history – my mother bought one new in 1971, I designed and prototyped a three-wheeled Mini-based kit car during the 1990s, and my last Mini in the UK was known as Old Scabby and yielded regular technical repair stories each time it broke down. It's now treasured by a friend's daughter and has been painted Ford 1600E purple and rechristened Lady Scabs.

I now run a Mini in Canada, known as Bubble because it's the colour of champagne and because it has a few bubbles in the paint. Minis in North America aren't just budget fun cars, though – they're rare, foreign, exotic, and valuable. Rather like running a '60s Lancia in the UK. For a sensible daily car I drive an immense but surprisingly economical 1958 Chevrolet with a 5.7-litre V8 from a Z28 Camaro, on which the tailfins are about the same length as a Mini. In fact I sometimes take my Mini with me in the boot. Less sensibly, I'm also manufacturing low-budget lightweight turbocharged Mazda MX5-based AC replicas under the Ayrspeed. com banner. I don't seem to be able to leave ACs behind. And I've just taken on a 1950 Roll-Royce project. Couldn't resist it.

Having recently driven a Mini Marcos halfway across Europe, I find I badly need one of those too. Fortunately they're still available as a new kit, and by the time I've finished this book I might even have made some progress with my Cunning Plan to race one at the Le Mans Classic. Race a Mini at Le Mans? What? The trouble with Mini-based eccentricity is that it's infectious. I've also recently driven a couple of Z-Cars Minis too, so of course I need one of those as well.

The Minis in this book range from barking mad to quite sensible in a psychotic sort of way. The owners all look and seem quite normal, and some of them even hold down conventional jobs. On the other hand, many of them, your humble narrator included, are completely unemployable.

Here's what some Mini enthusiasts did during their holidays.

↑An increasing number of people feel that a ten-foot-long four-seater Mini wastes too much space, so this is how they cure it. Not many cars will do a wheelie backwards…

↑Team Arse was one of the teams of Mini enthusiasts competing in deeply silly games at a typical Mini meet at the Hop Farm in Kent. Seen here undertaking the co-ordinated walking-the-planks. They're still sober, too.

↑The obsession with Minis doesn't just include full-size cars: concours judge Fiona Mannion's extensive collection of model Minis is fairly typical.

Minissan
God Save The Clown

↑ The dynamics of Minissan were unbelievably well sorted, straight out of the box. It only gets rude when you boot it.

→ At first glance the car still looks like a Mini. Retaining the chrome bumper helped with that.

GodSaveTheClown.com

Mike Guido may sway towards the madder side of the Mini continuum, but he also sometimes suffers from a very sane clarity of vision. He thinks that tobacco and alcohol companies marketing lethal drugs to children is a bad thing, morally not far from premeditated murder for financial gain. If you follow his logic, it's hard to argue with him: just reflect on the real purpose of alcopops. He decided to do something about it, and created an anti-drug campaign featuring The World's Fastest Clown. As the Clown, he got a factory ride with Nissan driving 240SX racing cars, but he drove them in full clown make-up and a fireproof clown suit. He says that gave him a real edge on the track: if he nudged somebody from behind and they looked in their mirror to see a clown grinning at them, it was really hard for them to concentrate on the next corner, which is all it would take for the Clown to get past.

The mad racing Clown then went to junior schools and put on an anti-drug magic show. As he's mad in a cool way, he got through to children where advice from parents and teachers never will, and he has probably saved a lot of young people from unpleasant, lingering but profitable deaths.

Nissan pulled out of racing, and the Clown resorted to competing in an innovative American budget race series where you're only allowed to spend a couple of grand on your car. In 2009 you're allowed to spend $2,009 on the car.

Minissan was originally intended for this, but instead it evolved into a show-and-go car that is now intended to attract as much attention as possible to get his campaign back on track, hence www. GodSaveTheClown.com on the windscreen.

Four years and 4,000 hours later, here it is. The shell is from 1962, and is the remains of Mike's first Mini that he couldn't bear to part with. The reason why it wandered so far off the true Mini path was to correct the two main dynamic deficiencies of the original Mini: the engines are too wee, and the drive is at the wrong end.

With enough money, you can persuade an A-series to kick out remarkable power, but 130bhp is only remarkable because the starting point is a little 1930s engine, and 350bhp from an A-series in practical and economical terms is simply not going to happen; whereas a second-hand Nissan V6 engine with cams and a nitrous bottle costs about the same as a week's holiday in Florida, which Mike doesn't need to pay for as he lives in Florida anyway.

The front-wheel-drive problem is even worse. More power and more acceleration means that more weight shifts to the back of the car, so there's even less weight on the front tyres, and you just get smoke and noise without much progress until the vehicle eventually collects enough forward speed for the tyres to stop spinning.

The front end geometry and suspension of Minissan remain related to Minis, but Mike had to learn a lot about steering and suspension theory to get the rack height perfect and avoid thumb-breaking bump-steer. He used a standard right-hand-drive Mini steering rack, which had to be mounted under the sump. Rack height is critical in any car, and getting it wrong results in bump-steer and vicious steering kick. He even got the Ackermann angle right, which is the degree to which the inner front wheel steers more than the outer front wheel when cornering. That angle is not critically important as it mostly means minor

← How many Minis have two spinning cam gears under the bonnet? The V6 fits in there very comfortably.

↑ Mike left some of the original spot welds in the shell just to prove the car is a real Mini.

GodSaveTheClown.com

← Much of the front end of the car could still be a Mini – there's no sign of its real character until you get near the back.

↓ The area of holes matches the area of the radiator fan, which blasts the heat out of the cooling system in seconds.

↑→ The interior fittings gleam. Everything is either black, red or gleaming polished metal, much of it stainless steel.

tyre scrub when parking, but it's revealing that he took the trouble to research it and sort it out. Mike's first crack at steering design beats TVR, who in 1967 were still building in rack-height bump-steer after designing cars for 20 years.

The rear end of Minissan took a solid month of work. When Mike does reluctantly spend time on his day job, he has to build adventure playground towers, platforms, rope bridges and so on. If he can slide out of work and spend

his days in the garage playing with mad Minis instead, he goes for that option every time. Minissan's rear end is the independent diff, shafts and subframe from a Nissan 240SX, narrowed by 12in. The half-shafts were each chopped by 6in: they're so short that the rubber boots are touching in the middle. Rear shock struts are 240SX front strut cartridges modified to work as rear struts, and the front shocks are from a Yamaha R6 bike. The springs are a massive 650lb front and 550lb rear, so it's weird that Minissan feels so drivable. It's also funny watching the car trying to get up a sloping driveway at the oblique angle required to avoid wrecking the front air dam: the car is so stiff that a wheel comes off the ground, and it's best to go up backwards and fast.

When power is dumped in, the back of the car is designed to squat a little to maximise grip. With Mike in the car, the front-to-back weight distribution is a virtually perfect 50% front, 50% back.

With a mid-front mounted V6 and independent rear-wheel drive, the original monocoque structure of the Mini was to some extent rendered irrelevant, and was replaced by a rollcage/spaceframe chassis that provided mountings for everything, which was constructed in and around the Mini shell. The body is not the usual decorative and detachable GRP shell found on most spaceframed Minis, it's the original steel body integrated with the cage, which passes through the body in several places. As much of the original Mini was used as possible – the Mininess of the car was important to Mike, contradictory though that may sound. The remaining inner wings still feature spot-welds from 1962.

I haven't seen another car of this type with this level of detailing: each of the welds that passes through the Mini shell was ground, sanded, wet'n'dried, guide-coated, primed, wet-sanded and finally covered in rich red paint.

There isn't anything else in the world quite this shape, so the fat wheel arches and other body panels had to be made from scratch. That meant mentally creating the shapes, then sketching them out, then fabricating them in 3D in the garage out of whatever material came to hand, then perfecting them, then duplicating the whole lot as mirror images for the other side of the car, then taking moulds and finally making the panels. It's making me tired just thinking about it.

Mike was paranoid about engine cooling, which was very sensible as the boot of a car is the worst possible place to put the radiator. There isn't a great deal of spare real estate under the bonnet, and Mike wanted to move some weight to the rear anyway. His response was overkill. The bootlid has more holes in it than global warming babble, the radiator is vast and the electric cooling fan is

18in in diameter. The fan is so powerful that it blew big fuses until sorted out. It now runs at half speed, which is more than enough. The cooling is amazing – on the car's first outing, a blown fan fuse allowed the engine to brew up. A replacement fuse was fitted to the circuit. When it was turned on, there was a blast of hot air out of the bootlid, which faded to warm and then cool air in about ten seconds, as the temperature gauge needle swivelled back to room temperature literally as you watched it.

The most remarkable thing about this car is the way it all worked straight out of the box. As ever with these projects, it was completed at 4:00am the night before its photo shoot. The car was taken off its jacks, fired up and driven down the street, and apart from the monster

↑ Early stages – sit in the car, build it around you.

↓ The elaborate frame in the back supports the independent rear axle and suspension.

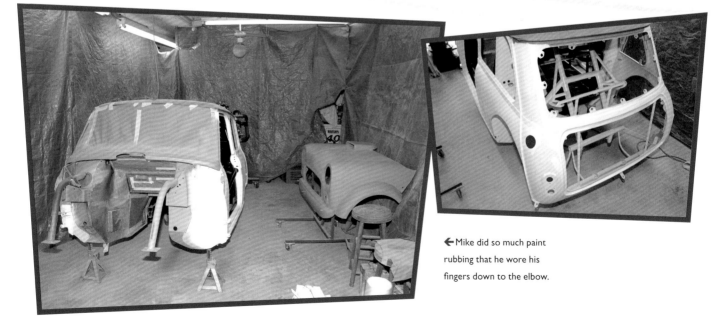

← Mike did so much paint rubbing that he wore his fingers down to the elbow.

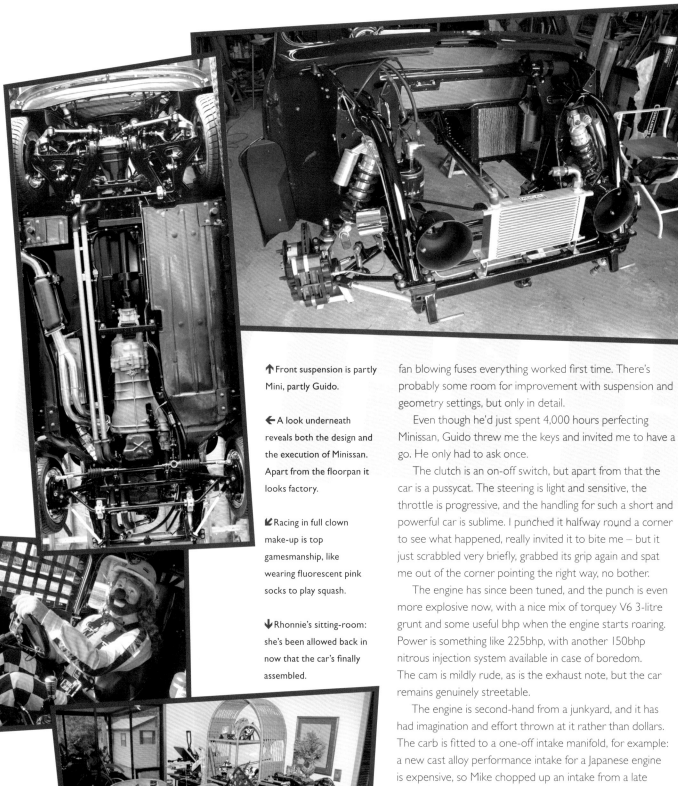

↑ Front suspension is partly Mini, partly Guido.

← A look underneath reveals both the design and the execution of Minissan. Apart from the floorpan it looks factory.

↙ Racing in full clown make-up is top gamesmanship, like wearing fluorescent pink socks to play squash.

↓ Rhonnie's sitting-room: she's been allowed back in now that the car's finally assembled.

fan blowing fuses everything worked first time. There's probably some room for improvement with suspension and geometry settings, but only in detail.

Even though he'd just spent 4,000 hours perfecting Minissan, Guido threw me the keys and invited me to have a go. He only had to ask once.

The clutch is an on-off switch, but apart from that the car is a pussycat. The steering is light and sensitive, the throttle is progressive, and the handling for such a short and powerful car is sublime. I punched it halfway round a corner to see what happened, really invited it to bite me – but it just scrabbled very briefly, grabbed its grip again and spat me out of the corner pointing the right way, no bother.

The engine has since been tuned, and the punch is even more explosive now, with a nice mix of torquey V6 3-litre grunt and some useful bhp when the engine starts roaring. Power is something like 225bhp, with another 150bhp nitrous injection system available in case of boredom. The cam is mildly rude, as is the exhaust note, but the car remains genuinely streetable.

The engine is second-hand from a junkyard, and it has had imagination and effort thrown at it rather than dollars. The carb is fitted to a one-off intake manifold, for example: a new cast alloy performance intake for a Japanese engine is expensive, so Mike chopped up an intake from a late 1980s throttle body injected Nissan pickup and started modifying that instead. He welded a Holley spacer plate to the top of it and then ported and polished it, then had it ceramic coated. It's probably within a few bhp of a seriously expensive performance item, but the price was paid in skill and patience.

Mike knows from experience that the stock Nissan V6 can handle up to 450bhp, so it can definitely take a joke.

Even with the nitrous, the engine is well within its limits, and even if he got a lot more cheeky with this engine and blew it up, a replacement would only cost a few hundred bucks.

Remarkably, the entire budget for Minissan was around four grand in pounds, because of the car being originally conceived for low-budget racing. Most of the money has been spent on paint and chrome plating, so it's 4,000 hours of hard graft you're looking at, not a chequebook street rod.

Mike's wife Rhonnie has been behind him all the way, including making the carpets, hand-polishing several hundred little stainless steel screws, helping lay the fibreglass moulds and final pieces, and putting up with her kitchen and house crammed full of Minissan bits for several years: so she absolutely deserves the shorty Mini she's been promised.

The Clown has been unable to get enough funding or official support for his drug prevention campaign in America, as the less effective but more conventional programmes are firmly in place: the individual towns and schools to which he has taken his show always ask him back, though.

If he got the opportunity to bring his campaign to British children he'd be happy to do so. If you're able to put The World's Fastest Clown in a professional motor racing series and into schools, get in touch with Mike at mike@worldsfastestclown.com. American parents may lack the imagination and commitment for this, but perhaps the Brits can do better? It wouldn't do any harm to British companies' media profile either, come to think of it.

ENGINE – Nissan 300ZX VG30 2998cc V6, steel block, alloy OHC heads. Lightened harmonic balancer, Schneider cams with 0.427in lift, 270 duration, advanced 3°. MSD Digital 6 distributor with magnetic pickup, NGK plugs, Accel leads, Holley 350CFM two-barrel carb with K&N filter on modified throttle body injection inlet manifold from 1980s Nissan truck. Standard ceramic-coated exhaust manifolds, single 12in silencer, 150bhp nitrous oxide system, Mocal 18-row oil cooler, 19in x 27in x 3in radiator with 18in electric fan. Holley 7psi race fuel pump, 100amp Mini alternator, aluminium flywheel, ACT 6-puck race clutch.

TRANSMISSION – 1990s 300ZX five-speed manual gearbox. Narrowed independent Nissan 240SX diff, driveshafts and subframe with viscous LSD, 4:1 final drive ratio.

SUSPENSION – Front, Mini subframe with 1.5in removed from towers. Standard upper arms, 1.5° negative camber lower arms, HD adjustable tie rods. Yamaha R6 monoshocks with 650lb springs. 0.75in adjustable anti-roll bar. Rear, ex-240SX front Koni strut cartridges, modified. SPL rose-jointed upper and toe arms, aluminium uprights, 550lb springs. 0.75in adjustable anti-roll bar.

BRAKES – Mini pedal box, Geo Metro (Chevrolet) master cylinder and servo. Adjustable front/rear bias. Handbrake from 1967 Austin-Healey Sprite, cables from 240SX. Front, Outlaw four-pot aluminium calipers with 9in vented discs, Performance Friction pads. Rear, 240SX non-vented discs.

WHEELS AND TYRES – All Diamond steel. Road wheels: front, 7J x 13 with Sumitomo HTR200 175/50 x 13; rear, 7J x 15 with Sumitomo HTR50Z 205/50 x 15. Race wheels: front, 8J x 13 with Hoosier 225/40 x 13; rear, 8J x 15 with Hoosier 225/45 x 15.

INTERIOR – Aluminium race seat, five-point Safe Quip racing harness, custom cage, Smiths oil pressure, water temp, fuel pressure in custom pod. Auto Meter tacho, water temp warning, MSD shift light. Hurst gear lever. Brake bias handle. Detachable steering wheel. Detachable nitrous bottle and frame alternate with Rhonnie's passenger seat and harness.

EXTERIOR – Fibreglass doors and flip front, home-made flares/air dam/side scoops/bootlid/bonnet scoop.

← With four years of design and construction out of the way, it's time for some fun on dragstrips and racing circuits.

The Suicide Chop

Jason Neumann was headed for a career in graphic design, and to pay his way through college he worked at a Costco wholesale supermarket. Trouble is, Costco liked him and kept giving him more money, so by the time he finished his degree he would have had to take a stonking pay cut to start being a designer.

As he enjoys the good things in life such as food and having a house to live in, Costco won. However, you can't keep artists down, as their ideas will emerge in another form – and after four years of imagination and application, this Mini is the result.

The shell is a 1963, but it was only a shell, so all he knows is its date and that it was an Austin. Could be it was an 850, possibly a Cooper S – but in its current form it's certainly transcended its original purpose during Jason's metamorphosis of it.

The roof had already been chopped by 4in when Jason bought the car as a rusty shell, but hadn't been chopped very well. It needed considerable work, so he decided to get radical and fit a big glass sunroof out of a BMW Mini while he was at it. In the end he cut a large chunk of the roof off a BMW Mini and welded that into the Mini shell, which in itself must have taken a while. This gave the roof a flatter look than the usual rather domed Mini roof panel, and made the car look even lower. It also allows Jason to drive it in the 100° Florida summer without air conditioning, which would otherwise be pretty brutal.

There was much grunt work in this project before anything creative could take place: the shell was de-seamed, which if done properly means many, many hours of patient work. The strength originally provided by the exterior seams needs to be replaced with more welded steelwork along every inch of the seams, or the structure ends up with the strength of a wet paper bag. The front wings also needed to be extended, and Jason chose the best but most difficult approach, which is to cut them in half at the arch tops and add sheet metal in the middle.

Body stiffness loss from de-seaming was not a risk here anyway, as Jason made a ten-point rollcage from steel tubing that connects the front and rear subframes and the body. Rigidity in this car is not going to be a problem.

The doors and bootlid are shaved, which with this level of paintwork is in itself a big job, as it means replacing holes and door-handle dips with new metal so that the change is invisible. Thick blobs of filler just won't cut it.

More than that, the doors and bootlid all open the wrong way. Changing ordinary MkI doors to rear-hinged suicide doors isn't too bad a job because the geometry of the opening angle is relatively simple, but a side-opening bootlid has to swing directly outwards before it starts turning, and the geometry of that can get weird. I ran into that problem designing bootlid hinges for replica Jaguar XK120s, and it was a bitch. Jason had to scratch-build hinges with sketches, cardboard templates and finally steel, but the result rewards his efforts – the bootlid fits a treat. Of course, it helped that he filled all the door and panel gaps, block-sanded the whole thing and recut the gaps to

← My first front-cover shot for *MiniWorld*. Much location hunting to find the right alleyway, then a two-hour wait for the sun to arrive at the right place.

→ The bonnet is the only panel on Jason's car that opens the way you would expect it to.

finer tolerances. Which, as you can imagine, took a while.

Some nice touches include the rear lights, which you can't see. Not until they're lit, anyway: they're just thin strips cut in the bodywork and filled with translucent red lighting plastic the same colour as the paint. They were heated into shape, pushed through the holes to stick up proud by quarter of an inch, then rubbed down flat with the body and finally lacquered over after painting to make them more or less disappear. Very cool, that. The rear window is also plastic – it's unbreakable Lexan. It's unbreakable but not unscratchable, and has to be polished rather than cleaned. The glass front screens tend to crack when cut down, and it was Jason's penultimate screen that survived: he now only has one spare.

The front end is also quite dramatic, and involved interesting styling choices as well as subtle but extensive fabrication. The front wings are extended slightly by 2in, and the front bulkhead would no longer be familiar to a Mini owner. The bonnet scoop is from a Toyota 4-Runner pickup truck, and the front bumper is an amalgam of various shapes, blended together and finished as a moulding buck, then moulded and reproduced.

The door inners were constructed using the same technique, so Jason can make more of any of the scoops,

front panel, dashboard or door inners if you like the look of them (jaynu@aol.com).

The dashboard was also made in the same way, with wood, chicken-wire, plastic foam gloop, whatever, then a mould was taken, then out came a silky smooth final panel of even thickness, ready to paint. Jason estimates that the dash and door panels took 500 hours…

The mad but brilliant gauges on stalks are a combination of bits of plumbing pipe and top graphic imagination. Having the steering on the right isn't anglophilia gone mad: right-hand drive just made it much easier to get everything in because the bulk of the Honda engine is on the left side of the engine bay, looking at the car from the back. There is a massive sound system, but it's just for the show stage of the car's career, and the speakers will probably be replaced by a back seat before too long.

That candy pearl paint job is quite a big deal. It's not really paint as such – it's more like lightly tinted clearcoat or varnish. The base coat is a gold metallic, and then the coats of House of Kolor Brandywine Kandy start being laid on. It takes many, many coats of it to get a colour this deep, and each of those coats has to be flawless. If that weren't tricky enough, there's pearl in there as well, and pearl paint is much worse than ordinary metallic paints for not matching.

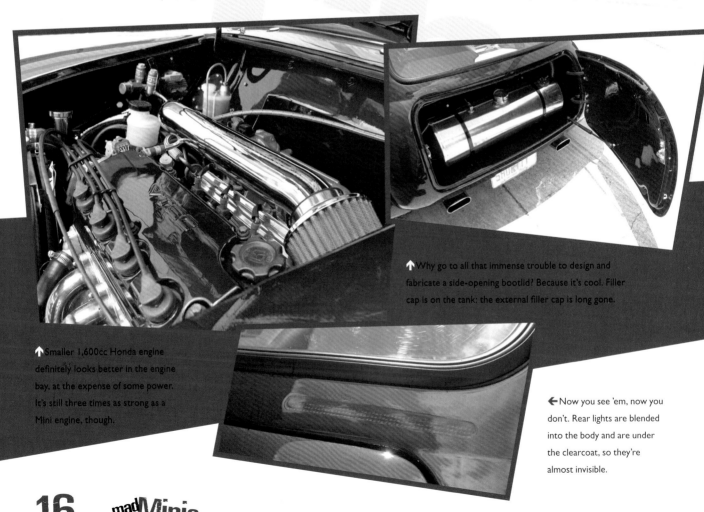

↑ Why go to all that immense trouble to design and fabricate a side-opening bootlid? Because it's cool. Filler cap is on the tank: the external filler cap is long gone.

↑ Smaller 1,600cc Honda engine definitely looks better in the engine bay, at the expense of some power. It's still three times as strong as a Mini engine, though.

← Now you see 'em, now you don't. Rear lights are blended into the body and are under the clearcoat, so they're almost invisible.

You really have to paint the whole car and all its panels at the same time, which means all holes masked off and the doors and panels mounted on stands, centrally supported – if you hook them up in the usual way, the hooks will disrupt the paint spray pattern and the anomaly will be visible. The surface needs to be prepped and completely dust-free between each coat too. As you can see from the pics, Jason managed to achieve the state of stubborn, anal-retentive obsession necessary to get the paint right.

The choice of a smaller Honda engine, the 1.6-litre single-cam rather than the usual 1.8-litre twin-cam, was a matter of both physical size and prettiness. That smaller 1,600cc Honda Vtec engine will go into a standard Mini front end, and it doesn't have to be jammed in, although it has to be said that the alternator was repositioned and an inch was cut off the tubular stainless exhaust manifold. Even so, the manifold position made Jason change from left-hand to right-hand drive just to make sense of the engine bay. It had to look good as well as being functional. The intake pipe was custom-made to pull cooler air into the engine, clear of the radiator. A detail, but worth a few extra horsepower.

The 1,600 looks a lot more visually comfortable in there than the bigger 1,800cc versions of the engine, and there are plenty of surface pieces on the engine available to be painted in the same colour as the body. If you're used to an A-series, going from 1,000cc and 50bhp to a Honda with 1,600cc and 150bhp is going to be a fairly dramatic change even if you leave the engine standard, but of course Jason didn't leave it standard.

Tuning Honda engines is a different world from tuning the Mini's A-series, but LCBs and Swiftune are just changed for VAFCs and Apexi. The principles remain the same, though – get more air in and out, match the fuel supply to the air supply and away we go. The engine bay was designed to leave room for a turbo, which will make it quite nippy. Even with this level of planning there were issues: with the shell painted and the engine in, Jason's intended big radiator wouldn't fit and had to be substituted for a stock Honda rad. Fortunately it can handle the job, no prob.

Jason's engine is a Vtec, which has variable cam profiling to give a shopping cam for supermarket action at 1,200rpm, and a race cam for track day action at 7,000rpm. With a heavy Honda shell the cam profile change isn't too brutal, but in a Mini it chucks you half off the road, so Jason used an Apexi Vtec controller. This allows you to bring in the Vtec effect lower down the rev

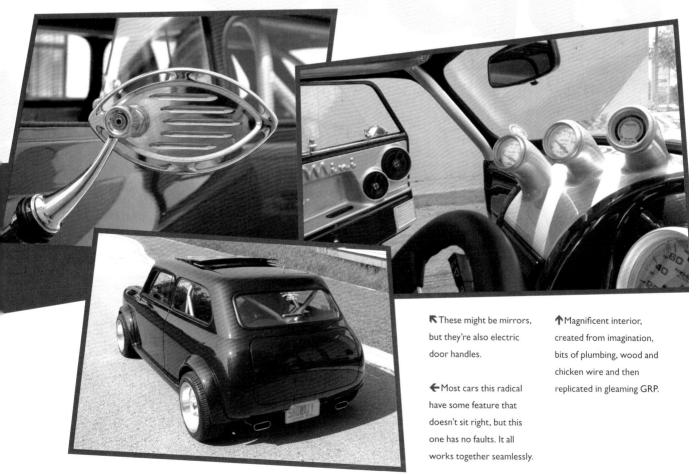

↖ These might be mirrors, but they're also electric door handles.

← Most cars this radical have some feature that doesn't sit right, but this one has no faults. It all works together seamlessly.

↑ Magnificent interior, created from imagination, bits of plumbing, wood and chicken wire and then replicated in gleaming GRP.

↑ Roof chop gives the car an uncompromising attitude. Removing the gutters usually makes Minis look bald, but in this case it works. Flat BMW sunroof helps.

↓ New front subframe was custom-built around the engine to get it all in without looking too crowded.

← The bumper buck was constructed from bits of different air dams blended into one and then reproduced.

← Door mouldings were scratch-built, entirely to Jason's design.

range where its kick is less nasty, and allows more control over fuelling, making it easier to match the fuel supply to the extra air coming in through the uprated air filter and intake. There are also bigger injectors from an 1,800cc engine. All of this is good sense and sound tuning practice, and the result according to Jason should be about 150bhp at the crank: that sounds reasonable. There's much more still to go into the engine later – plans include a Gude cam and cam gear – but the engine is very amusing as it is.

One side effect of the fairly brutal cam profile change is that the engine moved too far on its original mountings for the clearances available. It's okay if it flaps about in a Honda shell as there's plenty of room, but in the small Mini engine bay it had to be kept tied down tighter, with stiff custom engine mounts. That's even with the mods Jason made to the bulkhead to give himself clearance to work on the engine. The stiff engine mountings have added to vibration and cabin noise, but it can't be helped.

The Honda motor is bigger than the A-series but is all aluminium, so it doesn't upset the car's weight balance too much. The NOS system is really just there to frighten people: it's not really part of Jason's approach.

It's an interesting thought that the old A-series Mini engine tops out at about 130bhp, which is about where the smaller Honda engine bhp numbers begin.

The gearbox is a stock Honda five-speed, and as a Mini fanatic from way back, Jason enjoys upgrading to one-finger Japanese gearchanges and the additional cog. The uprated clutch master cylinder and ultra-lightweight JUN flywheel sharpen up the gear changes to match the engine's general tight feel, and sticking with the original Mini rubber cones, although tamed to some extent by Spax adjustable shocks, means the hard ride also matches the hard engine.

Freeway speeds in the USA reflect the lack of speed-tax cameras, and 80mph is usual. A Mini engine makes a fair old racket cruising at 80mph, and Jason does enjoy the luxury of changing up into fifth gear without handing over several grand for a custom A-series five-speed. He also enjoys the 40mpg+ cruising economy provided by the combination of the five-speed, the low aerodynamic profile and the car's weight of 1,000lb less than the donor Honda.

He doesn't enjoy the ferocious steering kick so much – the driveshafts are part-Honda and part-Mini, and the rest of the suspension and the brakes are either Mini or Metro – after all, if it ain't broke don't fix it, and Mini suspension design definitely ain't broke. It all works rather well considering that it was designed for 34bhp rather than 150bhp. The nitrous oxide system is for real, but has never been used: it would certainly provide some bicep-building torque steer if it was turned on.

One of the cool things that he and everybody else enjoys is opening the doors. With the handles shaved,

ENGINE – 1.6 Honda Vtec SOHC, with 1.8 Integra injectors, MSD distributor cap, MSD SS coil, APEXi valve-timing controller, high-flow air filter and intake, FAL Performance cooling fan. Nitrous oxide injection system. Shortened and re-welded stainless exhaust manifold, custom twin-tailpipe exhaust. Custom air intake pulls cool air. Gude cam and cam gear due soon, currently about 150bhp at the crank with nitrous switched off. Custom front subframe and engine cradle.

TRANSMISSION – JUN ultralight flywheel, Stage Three clutch and master cylinder. Honda 1.6 Vtec gearbox, standard with shortened gear linkages. Honda/Mini custom driveshafts.

BRAKES – System, Geo Metro (US car) master cylinder and servo. Stainless braided lines. Front, Metro Turbo vented four-pot. Rear, Cooper S drums.

SUSPENSION – Rubber cone, with adjustable Hi-Los. Spax adjustable shocks all round.

WHEELS AND TYRES – Superlite deep dish 7J x 13, with Yokohama 175/50 R13 tyres.

INTERIOR – Cobra seats, retrimmed with Mini logos. Ten-point handmade rollcage connecting both subframes, Auto Meter gauges and shift light, custom GRP dashboard and door trims, electric door opening via mirrors, Sony flip CD, Earthquake 3,000W amp, two Earthquake 12in BBX-12DR bass speakers, two 6.5in and two 5.75in MB Quart high end speakers.

EXTERIOR – 4in roof chop, 2005 BMW Mini electric glass sunroof, suicide doors, de-seamed shell, shaved rear lights, door handles, filler neck and bootlid, custom side-hinged bootlid, recessed licence plate mount, flush rear strip lighting, extended front wings and bonnet, Toyota bonnet scoop, one-off GRP front air dam/bumper, House of Kolor Brandywine Kandy paint.

➔ Jason's car is cotton-budded perfection at the moment, but is also designed for practicality and performance when he gets bored with winning show prizes.

door and bootlid operation is electric, and the doors are operated by pushing the door mirrors down, at which point the doors click and pop open.

Jason's car was built mostly as a sculpture, and mostly to win awards, which it has done with tremendous success. However, it was also built to provide a bundle of more active fun once the initial impact had quietened down, and he will gradually begin to use the Mini rather than show it: he just has to accept that the paint job that

took hundreds of hours of rubbing will collect more road rash and scratches the more fun he has with the car. Some sort of better rear lighting is also going to have to be devised, as the cool rear light strips look wonderful but don't actually work very well. Unlike some Honda installations, the oil filter location was designed to be easily accessible: Jason expects to be changing the oil quite frequently as the years go by, particularly when the matching Mini trailer has been constructed.

Chuck's Fire Engine

BEXLEY
HEALTH AUTHORITY

At the 2003 All British Field Meet in Van Dusen Gardens in Vancouver, Canada, an elderly expat Brit looked at a Mini, went white and stepped back in amazement. As well he might: he'd more or less seen a ghost.

In around 1968, in Bexley Hospital, England, he'd been the driver of this little red Mini-based fire engine.

Fast-forward to 2003, through an emigration and 35 years, and he was wandering around a classic British car show in Canada admiring some nice pre-war Bentleys and Austins, when he came across the very same fire engine. It had been imported into Seattle, USA, a while back, and had been taken up to Vancouver for the weekend to be displayed at the show by members of the Vancouver Mini Club.

It seems extraordinary that it had survived unrestored for this length of time, but it does make sense when you think about it. The reason there are so many ancient fire engines still around is that they have a pretty easy life. Unless something's on fire, they just sit in a shed. They're serviced, given a little gentle exercise now and again to keep them running, given an annual MOT test and then put back in the shed. This particular vehicle probably didn't see much firefighting action – the main reason it existed was that Bexley Hospital was of a size that meant it was required to have its own fire tender because it was some distance from the nearest fire station. I reckon they would just have called 999 if they smelled smoke.

For 31 years, the Mini Firefly sat in its shed, accumulating mileage at the recorded rate of 51 miles per annum. Its present mileage reading is 1,592.8. The speedo is currently broken, so there may have been a few more miles – who knows?

The Firefly's origins go back 1,600 miles and 40 years to the Angus Fire Armour company, whose London Fire Engine and Sprinkler Department announced a brand new 'compact and capable fire-fighting unit', the Mini-based Firefly. With an optional ladder (sadly lost many years back), pump, water tank, hose, ladder gantries and rear canvas roof or tilt, the converted pickup retailed for the grand total of £829. The Mini-based fire engine was a new concept, but the Angus Firefly was an established brand:

← The doors weren't originally signwritten, but somebody has had some magnetic Bexley Health Authority decals made. It should logically be Bexley Illness Authority, shouldn't it?

↓ The pump, hose and tank fit neatly. Hauling a steel tank containing 50 gallons of water would be hard going for an 850, you'd have thought.

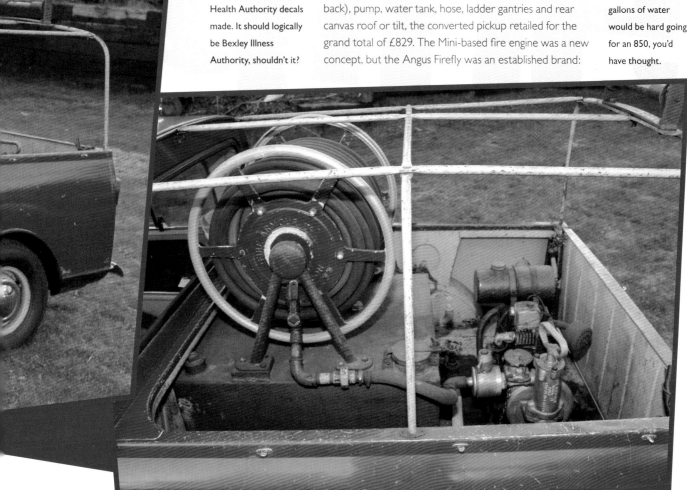

←Chuck Heleker displays the fire axe and hand-held extinguisher supplied with the Firefly.

↑The Winkworth electric bell is currently defunct, but Chuck will eventually get it working and annoy his Seattle neighbours with it.

the 1960 Angus Firefly was the same sort of design, but based on a Series II 109in Land Rover.

The big nobs at Bexley Hospital, Dartford Heath, Bexley, Kent, saw the demonstrator and what was possibly also the prototype Mini Firefly at the British Fire Services Association Conference at Hastings, and they liked the look of it. They asked for a brochure on 16 January 1964, ordered their Firefly on 20 February, and took delivery in June. For the next 31 years the Firefly pottered around the hospital, occasionally extinguishing a dustbin fire but mostly parked in its shed.

In 1995 it was sold, and any dreams of the open road that it might have had were dashed. Its new British owner registered it and then stored it. Three years later, Seattle Mini enthusiast Chuck Heleker bought it and shipped it from the UK to the Pacific Northwest, where it arrived in February of 1998. The engine still ran, but neither the hydraulics nor the tyres were safe to drive at anything more than walking speed. Chuck describes the brakes as a 'dual leaking shoe design'.

In the twelve years since then, has the old fire truck tasted freedom and the highway and put some miles under its belt? No … it's been stored in the back of Chuck's basement garage with his other 13 assorted Minis.

'What are you going to do with it?' I asked.

'You know, that's a real tough call…' said Chuck.

He's not yet at all sure what to do with the little fire engine, although it's high on his list of treasured possessions. It only has two seats and the back is full of hose, water

tank and pump, so it's not really of much practical use. It's also quite heavy and only has an 850cc engine, so driving it could be fairly hairy on Seattle's 80mph freeways.

Chuck doesn't want to restore the Firefly because that would spoil it. The likely outcome is that when he has some spare time and money, he'll get the engine going properly, overhaul the hydraulics and fill them with silicone fluid, and then just take it out and play with it sometimes. If the hydraulic system is all new, there are unlikely to be problems with swollen seals, and with no hygroscopic brake fluid sucking water into the system there will be no further rust in the brake and clutch cylinders. Maybe Chuck will even finish off running the engine in. Of course something may catch fire some day, in which case it could be very useful to have a fire engine in the middle of the workshop.

One thing that he definitely wants to do is take it to a few fire engine shows. He's not a particular fire engine enthusiast himself, but lots of people are, and they'd definitely love to see it.

The pump works fine: again, it hasn't seen a great deal of action. It's fixed to the pickup bed, but has handles at either end. It was originally designed to be manhandled to a stream or a source of water and then it was supposed to pump water straight from there to the fire. There's a 50-gallon water tank in the pickup bed which would only just be enough to put out a dustbin fire. The hose is probably not the 1964 original, as it still looks serviceable, if elderly.

There may or may not have been a pair of lockers inside

the pickup bed. The brochure shows them but the Firefly doesn't have them.

The chrome-plated brass Winkworth bell was not specified in the original invoice: the Firefly was supposed to have had a 'Du Flash Syren' fitted, but presumably that packed up and was replaced by the electric bell. Which has now also packed up. Chuck expresses no surprise that elderly British wiring on a Mini fire engine bell doesn't work any more, although to be fair, the rest of the Lucas electricals do still seem to work unexpectedly well.

There isn't much known about these little fire engines, other than that there were at least two built – the

prototype and this one. Chuck would be fascinated to hear if anybody has any more information, and he would be over the moon if anybody could replace his missing ladder.

Chuck is busier than ever, either fixing Minis or driving them mad distances around America. So the fire engine is still on the lower rungs of his ladder of priorities. Another few years in storage for the Firefly, then.

Chuck would like to talk to the chap he met in Vancouver, whose name may have been Dave Harmer… he has a note reminding him to call, but no number. If anybody knows Dave, Chuck can be contacted via www.SeattleMiniOwners.com.

← … and a bargain at 829 pounds, no shillings and no pence.

↓ KR is a Kent registration. From January 1963 most local councils issued number plates with an A suffix for 1963 and a B suffix for 1964. After 1964, year suffix letters were mandatory.

Tech

ENGINE – Standard 848cc, SU HS2 carb.
TRANSMISSION – Standard four-speed.
IGNITION – Standard points/condenser.
BRAKES – Standard drums all round.
WHEELS AND TYRES – 3.5in steels, with replacement 145 x 10 tyres. Original wheels have possibly the original tyres, now disintegrating.
INTERIOR – Stock original, with additional fire axe and hand fire extinguisher.
EXTERIOR – Fire Brigade Red over original Westminster Beige. Modifications: bell and wiring; ladder gantries; Villiers water pump; 50-gallon water tank; fire hose and reel.

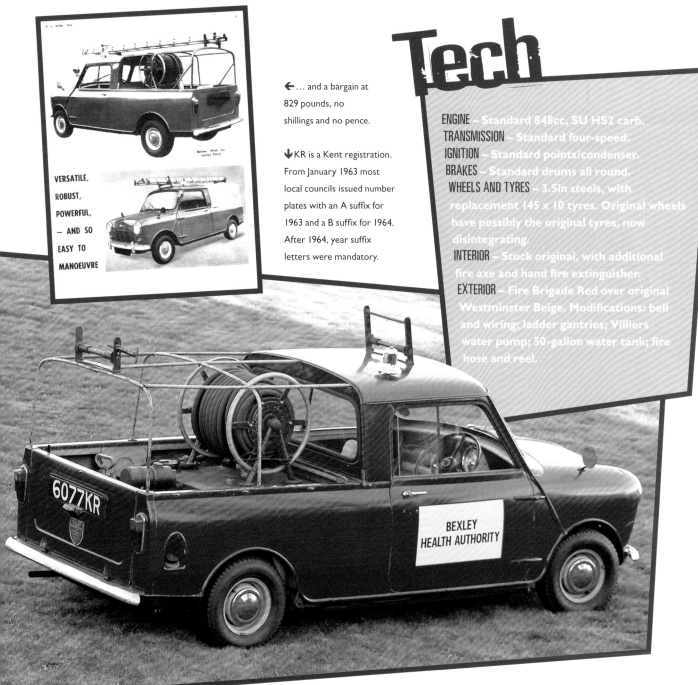

VERSATILE,
ROBUST,
POWERFUL,
— AND SO
EASY TO
MANOEUVRE

6077KR

BEXLEY HEALTH AUTHORITY

Orange and Juicy

Mark Heller is a retired US Navy bosun, which is the rank between those giving orders and those carrying them out. He's the guy who gets things done. As you can imagine, retiring to potter about in the garden and complain about the youth of today did not appeal to such a man, so he built a mad Mini instead.

He has a history of messing about with British cars, as his father was an engineer and a Brit-car enthusiast, although he didn't usually own a car. The Heller family lived in central Brooklyn, New York, and even 60 years ago good public transport and limited parking space meant there was no need for one. Mark learned to drive in an ancient Frogeye Sprite, and has owned a good few British cars, including a Humber Super Snipe. He liked its walnut and leather, and its general ambience. He also had a Hillman Imp, which he thought was an excellent design but a horrible car. A top buy was a Sunbeam Tiger, basically an Alpine with a 5-litre Ford V8, and one of the undervalued gems among British classics. That particular car has been replaced by his current Austin-Healey replica, which is a Corvette in a Healey-shaped frock supplied by Sebring – a company whose descendants still make Healey replicas today in Norfolk. Mark also likes grotesquely huge cars as well as tiny ones, and owns a stretch Cadillac limo and a Cadillac hearse that

has been converted to a mobile bordello with a crushed velvet interior and clinking crystal glasses.

One of Mark's major regrets, and the underlying reason for the existence of his mad Mini, is that he sold the 1967 Cooper S he bought new and later traded in. He regretted that decision for years, but he says he didn't inherit any of his father's talent for engineering, and as a non-mechanic he doesn't have the confidence to drive a 40-year-old genuine Cooper. Being a gentleman he put this politely, but he remembers that reliability was not the most notable attribute of British cars even when they were 40 years newer, so the idea of creating a Mini with a big and reliable Japanese engine appealed. 34bhp Minis are lots of fun, but it has to be said that 195bhp Minis are even more fun, and 195bhp Minis with Japanese engines that start up every day and don't throw a wobbly when it rains are maximum fun.

Mark took his concept to a local rod shop run by Dennis la Monte, who thought it would be a bit of a challenge and would make a nice change from building big-block V8 street and strip Mustangs, and who made an excellent job of realising Mark's plans. Finding the right Mini to work with was tricky, as Mark really didn't want to cut up a good one. After much scratching around,

← ← At first glance this just looks like a Mini with fat wheels.

↓ Looking at the back, the sheer size of the wheels becomes clear – it's not possible to fit anything bigger than 13in wheels with low profile tyres on a standard Mini.

↑ Looking up into the roof you can see some of the massive rollcage that is an extension of the chassis.

→ Plenty of engine info, air conditioner outlets and the head unit for the sound system.

↑ The depth of the front spoiler conceals the ride height of the car: if it just had a thin chrome bumper it would look like a monster truck.

a suitable car showed up in Deland, Florida, only half an hour away from his house in Daytona Beach. It was sunk into a garden, as rotten as an election promise, and the engine was shot as well. He licked his lips and made a suitable offer for it as scrap.

In some ways he would have liked to put the engine in the front, and it is possible to squeeze the Honda engine into the front end of a Mini, but unless you're really obsessed with retaining a standard front end the usual routine is to extend the front wings and bonnet, which didn't appeal to him. There's very definitely no room for air conditioning as well, though, and Mark lives in Florida where the temperature and humidity get pretty extreme. Okay then, if he wanted to keep the standard-length Mini front end, the engine would have to go in the back.

The Mini was stripped to the outer shell with the crumbled floor completely cut out, and a frame was constructed that would fit under the body. It made sense to leave the body unstressed and make the chassis more or less drivable on its own, because of the small space available inside the Mini shell. Being able to fit and remove the body would save time and trouble during the build.

The body kit around the edges of the Mini is British – if you check out the front shot closely you'll see the space left for the large British-sized plate. Florida law doesn't require a front licence plate, which makes a lot of sense. Not many criminals reverse away from the scene of a crime: even crims have realised that cars go better when facing forwards. The only use for front number plates

is speed-tax cameras, which in my view are verging on criminal themselves. Automobile bumf is pretty user-friendly in Florida: this car is titled as a 1974 two-door Austin Mini, with no requirement for inspection or emissions. Mark's Corvette-based kit car is a 1961 Healey, no worries. Much of Florida is pretty relaxed: the restaurant health inspector gets a welcome, a beer, a pizza and some NASCAR chat, and hey, this place looks clean enough.

Even with the engine occupying the whole back end of the car, getting everything jammed inside the bodywork was a challenge. 'You know how it is with Minis,' says Mark, 'every inch is accounted for.'

The chassis was constructed to use the front suspension and brakes from a 1999 Honda Prelude, and the rear end is the complete package from a '99 Integra. Because the rear end is now a front end, it comes with steering – but the way to deal with that is to throw away the steering rack and make solid brackets on the chassis, replicating the trackrod ends' geometry. The ex-trackrods are then attached to the brackets and can be used to adjust the rear tracking rather than steering the wheels. One big advantage of using factory geometry, or of misusing it depending on how you look at it, is that details like anti-dive geometry and the rack height can remain correct. If the rack height is wrong, the steering will be horrible, and even a small error can generate vicious bump-steer and kickback that can break your thumbs. Shortening the wheelbase does mean a change

in the Ackerman angle, but as we've seen before, that can be calculated and corrected, and even if it isn't, all that happens is increased tyre scrub at low speeds.

One area which puts Mark's concept way ahead of most Minis dynamically is the rear engine and rear-wheel drive. Front-wheel drive is excellent for packaging and cheap manufacturing, but as far as performance goes it's crap.

The problem is weight transfer. As soon as a front-drive car accelerates hard, the weight moves to the back and the front wheels lose grip. Much tyre smoke: not much progress. Mark's car, on the other hand, squats, loads up the back tyres and shoots off like a rocket. No fuss, no tyre

↑ Looking at the back, the track is somewhat wider than a standard Mini.

→ Tasty custom paint job has pinstripes, marbling and a base orange colour bright enough even to be seen by centenarians in Cadillacs.

↓ The profile reveals that the Mini's bodywork has been kept to the original length.

radiator is front-mounted, and amazingly even with no engine in there the front boot or ex-engine bay is already full with the rad, the fuel cell and the brake and clutch hydraulics. Fuel cells for racing are a good idea for custom Mini builders – they come in assorted shapes and sizes, they have integral senders and fuel caps, and they do well in a crash.

The gear linkages were a real pain, as the whole mechanism had to be fabricated to work 180° the wrong way, and had to run along for 4ft under the engine in order for the gear lever to come up by the driver. The five forward gears work fine, but reverse has proved to be a problem: the car just sits there while assorted horrible crunching noises emanate from the gearbox. Like JZR Morgan replica trike drivers with only forward gears, Mark learned to avoid parking anywhere that involved reversing.

The brakes didn't prove to be a problem, but a new system had to be designed from scratch. The major issue here is that the car has two sets of front brakes, which is potentially a very dangerous mismatch – you need about 20% of braking going to the back wheels and 80% to the front. In the end a Chrysler master cylinder was used with some custom work on the Mini pedal to get the right leverage ratio, and it was easy to plumb in a brake-proportioning valve and set the pressure to go mostly to the front.

The Honda engine uses an electrical control unit and fuel injection, which led to complications – it's not as simple as recycling the wiring and throwing the Honda away. In the end, the ECU and the engine loom were persuaded to coexist with the rest of the electricals, and they run the engine just fine. There are eight separate fused circuits for accessories, and the wiring is otherwise standard Honda or rewired to a Mini diagram.

The Honda Vtec engine gets 195bhp partly because of variable valve geometry, so you effectively get different camshafts at different engine speeds. The Vtec cam has a shopping-car cam profile at idle, and extra locking lobes turn it into a monster cam at full chat. It's operated by engine oil pressure, but it's controlled by the ECU, as are the rest of the engine's functions – so without the computer, the engine is an ornament. Mark would have preferred carbs and points, but that engine wouldn't get anywhere near 195bhp without electronics.

Mark had his fun with this car, then passed it on to a rabid Florida Gators American Football fan who has added his own details. The colour scheme just happens to be exactly the team colours of the Gators. This is the kind of

squealing, it's just suddenly elsewhere. The 1,800cc Honda Integra package also comes with a limited-slip differential, which means the traction is as good as it gets. The Honda LSD can be quite brutal when fitted to the front of a Mini because of the lack of weight: but the weight at the back of Mark's Mini as it accelerates is quite a lot and loads the diff up nicely, so it just takes off in a straight line. The general handling's pretty good too, says Mark, although once the car gets out of line it tends to snap around and spin because of the rearwards weight balance and the short chassis. The suspension is still Honda, but the spring rates and shocks are designed to make the suspension much more hardcore Mini in feel than soggy Honda. There are also custom anti-roll bars front and back, so I'd suspect that Mark has to push this car pretty damn hard to get it to step out of line.

The wheels are enormous: they're 17in in diameter rather than the Mini's original 10in, which is why the car looks so much like a huge Hot Wheels toy. That's fine with Mark – a big toy is exactly what it is.

The Honda engine and gearbox mounts were recycled as well as the suspension geometry, keeping everything simple and reusing the standard mountings and bushes, so fitting the engine and box was very straightforward. The front and back ends of the chassis were connected by beams, and then an eight-point roll cage was built. The Mini shell was then lowered on to the chassis.

Where the rear seats used to be is now a carpeted box covering the engine and the air conditioning system, and the tunnel on the floor covers the radiator hosing, fuel and brake lines as they run to the front of the car. The

Tech

← Engine, transmission, suspension, driveshafts, hubs all bolt to the car's massively strong custom frame.

ENGINE – Honda Integra 1.8 DOHC Vtec B18 C5, standard, factory spec 195bhp at crank. Standard ECU spliced to custom/Mini wiring loom. Fabricated front-mounted cooling system with aluminium radiator. Fabricated exhaust manifold and exhaust, Supertrapp silencer on tailpipe. Remote fuel pump and filter, K&N air filter.

TRANSMISSION – Standard LSD Honda five-speed, with fabricated gear linkages and B&M short-throw gear lever. Fabricated chrome moly driveshafts.

BRAKES – Mini pedal box with altered pedal lever ratios and Chrysler master cylinder. Fabricated handbrake mechanism using additional calipers. Fabricated steel lines, front-to-rear adjustable balancing valve. Front, Honda Prelude discs and calipers with semi-metallic pads. Rear, Honda Integra discs and calipers.

SUSPENSION – Skunk Z Works adjustable coilover shocks all round. Fabricated front and rear anti-roll bars.

WHEELS AND TYRES – 8J x 17in TireWorld six-spokes with Pirelli P7000 225/35Z17 all round.

INTERIOR – Custom, with Honda Prelude seats narrowed by 2in and trimmed in blue vinyl, fabricated engine/air con system cover, centre tunnel, dashboard. Mountney steering wheel, Auto Meter Phantom gauge set, with 10,000rpm tacho and 160mph speedo. Autocraft harnesses. Custom trimming and dash.

EXTERIOR – Standard Mini shell, fabricated chassis and eight-point rollcage. Z-Max body kit reshaped to fit enlarged wheel arches and 17in wheels. Hella 130W headlamps. Paint, House of Kolor pearl orange, cobalt blue stripes with custom finish and pinstriping.

football where they run around for ten seconds wearing armour, then stop for commercials and for the cheerleaders to bounce about. Rather than British football where they run around for ten minutes then foul each other and fall over squealing and pretending they've got a broken leg.

The Magic Bus

After being involved in Mini trike endeavours as described later in this tome (Chapter 15), Alexander Fraser – Sandy to his chums – formed Lion Omnibuses and used the Mini mechanical package to power ⅔rd-scale drivable models of vintage lorries and buses. Among the more memorable ones were wartime AEC Matadors in Royal Air Force livery that were used to tow trailers full of visitors around Duxford aerodrome. Those were fitted with Mini engines, but longitudinally rather than transversely: the driveshafts went to live axles and diffs at either end and thus gave the Matador models four-wheel drive.

Some 40 of these assorted working models were made, and the bus featured is from the 1980s. Its purpose is to trundle slowly round summer fetes, loaded with screaming, sugar-buzzed children. Incidentally, I spotted a cool sign in a Vancouver bookshop recently that said 'Unaccompanied Children will be given a Double Espresso and a Puppy'.

The design of the bus is very practical for its purpose – the suspension is fairly stiff so there's little danger of the bus falling over, and the radiator is many times the size of a Mini one, constructed from rows of tubing like a condenser, and helped out by an electric fan: so it will amble around for hours at walking pace without brewing up.

The engine bay echoes with the emptiness of a cathedral, and the Mini engine lurks right down at the bottom. This particular engine turns out to be a standard 998, with a standard gearbox as well. The relatively huge and very convincing cast wheels result in some peculiar gearing: first gear feels like about third, and the bus is unlikely ever to go fast enough to use fourth.

← ← The proportions and detailing look spot-on. Who would ever expect Mini power?

← Elf'n'Safety would have something to say about the open deck and staircase if this were a commercial bus. Rear fog light looks daft but is legally required.

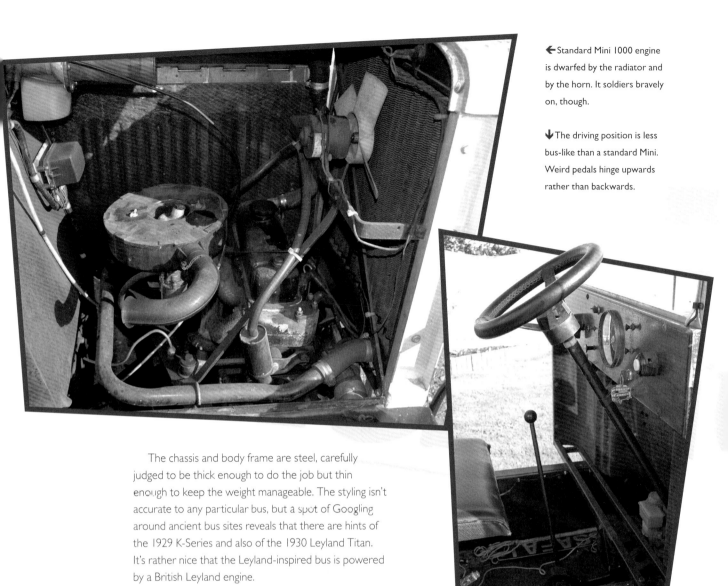

← Standard Mini 1000 engine is dwarfed by the radiator and by the horn. It soldiers bravely on, though.

↓ The driving position is less bus-like than a standard Mini. Weird pedals hinge upwards rather than backwards.

The chassis and body frame are steel, carefully judged to be thick enough to do the job but thin enough to keep the weight manageable. The styling isn't accurate to any particular bus, but a spot of Googling around ancient bus sites reveals that there are hints of the 1929 K-Series and also of the 1930 Leyland Titan. It's rather nice that the Leyland-inspired bus is powered by a British Leyland engine.

The more you examine it, the more the detailing pleases: Hammersmith to Liverpool St is genuinely the route of the No.11.

The bus is currently in the care of Chris Hollier of Stoke Ferry in Norfolk, the engineer who made the chassis and body of my own Mini-based three-wheeler: small world. It's kept MOT'd and street legal, and has a Q plate because it's a 'vehicle of indeterminate age'. It certainly fulfils that description.

Chris fires up the bus so that I can try it out, and there is a satisfactory amount of blue oil smoke: the engine is a little tired, which seems fair given the job it's been doing for 20 years. The gearbox is also tired, and the clutch is very weird. The pedals are now mounted horizontally, so you push them down rather than forwards. With crunching synchros and some very authentic whining from the gearbox, the bus ambles out on to Great Man's Way, the dead-end road Chris lives on, which is gradually sinking back into the fens, some parts faster than others. Slip the clutch to get going and

we lurch along, top deck leaning alarmingly, bell ringing furiously as the bus sways back and forth. Out on to a proper road and the ride is actually not bad. Floor it in first and wait for a while, have a chat, cup of tea, then eventually it's time for second gear. Time passes, Chris's children grow up, go off to work and get married, and by then the engine is finally revolving fast enough for third gear, and we're rolling now. Something of a queue forming behind, but hey ho. First and second gears are all you use most of the time, with third as an occasional treat. I try fourth just for fun, but it chugs unhappily and doesn't like it, way too high-geared even at the heady speed of 30mph.

Is this the most-obscure-ever vehicle powered by a Mini? It's certainly one of the most charming.

← The starting handle, although apposite, wouldn't have much effect on the transverse engine.

→ Cast ID plate says Lion Omnibus 87 CH 009, suggesting it's the ninth, built in 1987.

Lion Omnibuses
WHEN ORDERING RENEWALS
QUOTE NO
LION OMNIBUSES, 10 HIGH STREET
HORNING, SLEAFORD, LINCS
TELE 0529 240179

→ Chris is a big bloke, so he gives you some idea of what size the Mini-bus is.

Turbo Triple Miniac

6

Many old Minis run on three cylinders now and again, but only this one does it on purpose. Canadian Lyle Jansen didn't specifically set out to construct a Miniac from a Pontiac Firefly and a dead Mini: he was looking at various Japanese cars as potential donors for a Mini project that would be utterly different from any other Mini. This three-cylinder turbocharged rocket shopper just happened to turn up and seemed like an interesting option. Lyle's Minis are usually immaculate and standard, so this was definitely an aberration, but what a top aberration.

If you want to build a triple Mini as well, you don't need to hunt down a rare Canadian Pontiac Firefly Turbo Sprint. You can instead look for a Suzuki Swift, Maruti Swift, Geo Metro, Chevrolet Sprint, Maruti Esteem, Suzuki Cultus, Subaru Justy, Suzuki Forsa, Daewoo Kalos or just possibly a Holden Barima. BMC was in the forefront of badge engineering in the mid-'60s, with Austin or Morris Minis also available in Riley or Wolseley versions, and the larger and rustier 1100/1300 Pininfarina-styled saloon range available as Austin, Morris, Wolseley, Riley, Vanden Plas and even MG in the brief period between their construction and their disintegration. Suzuki have elevated badge bodgery to an art form.

Lyle is an automotive painter, restorer and fabricator by trade and by choice, and is one of those people so happy in his work he only stops for food and wine. When it's time to stop work he just says, yeah, whatever, eats some chips or something and then carries on until midnight.

He does have a 'proper' Mini as well, a standard round-fronted Mini Estate from 1970 with its correct A-series engine. It's now in gleaming red paint and slowly being assembled. Lyle has also worked on a couple of Vancouver Mini Club cars, as well as fellow Vancouver madman Rick Higgs's yellow Mini-and-trailer combo, also featured in this fine volume (Chapter 20).

Lyle's history includes British bikes and Harleys, Plymouth Roadrunners, big-block Chevelles, Corvettes and all sorts of serious and charismatic muscle, so your guess is as good as mine as to why he finished up with a turbocharged three-cylinder Mini.

Building custom cars for other people is fine, but Lyle wanted his own, and he was considering his options when he was offered a 1991 three-cylinder Pontiac Firefly Turbo. In standard form this is a slightly boring modern pocket rocket, but Lyle decided to combine it with a Mini shell to create something amusing, unique and also quite practical. It must be the world's first three-cylinder turbocharged intercooled Mini: anybody who knows different, let me know.

The beginning of the project was fairly simple – the Firefly engine was bored out by 60 thou, then rebuilt to standard spec for reliability. Taking the engine out is easy, as it's all-alloy and only has three cylinders anyway: Lyle just posted it off in a Jiffy bag for a rebuild.

↑When you look at the car from a different angle it just becomes more confusing. Is it a van? A fastback? Why would a van have a boot? What's going on?

←←From the front, Lyle's monster looks more or less like a Mini. The odd trim around the screen is because the latter was bonded in to add strength, rather than using traditional screen rubbers. Front end is a steel flip.

← The interior is mostly taken straight from the Pontiac, with the rest of it custom-made. The instrument binnacle is a good two feet further back than a Mini dash: you have to wriggle past it to get into the car.

↑ The entire mechanicals and floorpan are from the Pontiac. The lack of underbonnet shininess reflects daily use. EFI is multi-point, with separate injectors. The tiny turbocharger produces only limited horsepower, but the torque figure is quite good at 107lb/ft.

He then took an air chisel to the Firefly, cut it off at the ankles and threw most of it away above sill level. Next up for the *Brrrraaaap Brraaaaap* treatment with the air chisel came the Mini, which lost its entire floor structure and both subframes. Rust had already achieved most of that anyway, so it was largely a matter of cleaning what was left back to solid metal. When the skin of the Mini was lowered on to the Firefly floorpan, the Mini shell was 18in too short. No problem: he just cut it in half and chopped the roof off another scrap Mini to make up the difference. Lyle now admits he was a little hasty with the air chisel, as the original roof was cut too far back. Mini roofs actually have quite a pronounced crown, and the roof panels should ideally have been cut across the middle at the B-post to retain the original proportions.

As it happens, the final downwards-sloping slightly fastbacky look to the bodywork is part of its character – it's weird, but weird interesting rather than weird horrible… but doubtless everyone will have their own opinion. The amount and the quality of the steelwork is impressive. The rear windows have gone, plated over in sheet steel. To do that without visible wrinkles is not as easy as it sounds.

The flip front is also a labour of love, very neatly executed. The easy way out is a GRP flip front available by post for a few hundred bucks, but Lyle welded this one together from Mini panels, and designed and fabricated the necessary framework, hinges and detachable mounts. There's a lot going on under the bonnet, so fixed steel Mini wings weren't really a practical option for accessibility reasons. In any case, a smooth, well-made steel flip front really looks the business.

The back end of the Mini is just that, a standard rear end pressing and bootlid welded back on, but the rear panelling and the quarter-panels were fabricated from sheet steel, quite impressive work and a brave decision, as there's no way of disguising mistakes. Quite a lot of the Mini panels are new – it's much easier to build cars from new panels than to repair old ones.

The dash from the Pontiac was left in place and the Mini was then reconstructed around it. The dash is enormous and crammed full of stuff, and reaches way back into the Mini's cabin, which means you sit in what would have been the back seat. It's also rather fun that the driver is invisible – when the car's rolling it seriously looks as though there's nobody driving it, and the number of double-takes and dropped jaws is entertaining.

'It's not a Morris any more, but it's still a Mini,' says Lyle. 'People like it.'

The Wal-Mart plakky hubcaps are slightly embarrassing, but the Firefly's stud pattern is weird, and the available choices for it in North America are limited, nasty, and covered in cheap chrome, and mostly look worse than the hubcaps. Think loser pimp, think budget bling. Lyle will replace the wheels when something genuinely suitable turns up.

On the road, the independent suspension and the extra 18in on the wheelbase mean the ride is smooth and civilised, although the turbo whistle and blowoff-valve noises replacing the A-series gearbox whine sound pretty strange in a Mini.

There were no complications with changing the suspension to MacPherson struts at the front and multi-link at the rear, as the Pontiac's floorpan was retained as far up as the suspension mounts – Lyle just welded the Mini shell to the Pontiac pan and some of the substructure so that the stock suspension mounts were properly braced in the new structure, and left the geometry and mechanical components exactly as they came out of the Pontiac. The handling may not be as sharp as a proper Mini, but the trade-off in ride and comfort suits Lyle. The car is a daily driver and even tows a small trailer, so it has to work for a living and is not trailered to shows cradled in a nest of cotton buds and rose petals – it's a trailer truck rather than a trailer queen. The car's regular 40mpg

↑ The roofline on a Mini drops quite dramatically after the midpoint, which is why the rear end droops the way it does.

plus – even on smaller American gallons – is very useful in protecting Lyle's wine fund, Californian Fisheye Cabernet Sauvignon being his tipple of choice. He says the Miniac just seems to run on fumes rather than using any petrol to speak of.

'The power is about the same as a good 1275 Cooper S,' he says, 'and that's plenty.' Max power wasn't the point, or he'd have put a V8 in it. It's interesting to note the torque figure, which at 107lb/ft is good going for a small turbo engine and explains why the car drives so well: usually a small turbocharged engine is pretty feeble at low revs and only comes alive in the upper reaches of the tacho when the compressor is really screaming. Top speed is as yet untested, but even at licence-losing speeds there still seems to be plenty of power left.

The driving position is well weird, because the Pontiac's enormous dashboard containing the electronics was retained: the steering wheel has moved back 2ft from its original position, and so has the driving seat. Most of the time this works fine, as you just lean forward if you need to look out of a side window.

I'm keeping an eye on Lyle – I have no idea what he's going to do next, but it will probably top this.

Tech

ENGINE – 993cc three-cylinder all-alloy OHC multipoint fuel-injected Suzuki engine, RHB32 turbocharger with intercooler, bored out +60, 70bhp, 107lb/ft torque.

TRANSMISSION – Pontiac Firefly five-speed manual FWD transmission.

SUSPENSION – Complete floorpan from 1992 Pontiac Firefly Sprint Turbo. Front, independent with MacPherson struts, coils over, driveshafts through hubs. Rear, multi-link independent with MacPherson struts, separate coils, wide wishbones, additional stabilising arms.

BRAKES – Pontiac powered discs front, drums rear.

WHEELS AND TYRES – Standard Pontiac 4.5J x 13 steels, 165/65R13 Westlake H600 tyres. Wal-Mart plastic hubcaps: unusual PCD stud pattern limits wheel choice.

INTERIOR – Pontiac seats, entire dashboard, steering column, pedals. Rear deck constructed and trimmed, carpet-material headlining.

EXTERIOR – Mini sedan shell stretched 18in to fit Pontiac floor and wheelbase, rear window converted into van sides. Flip/detachable steel front constructed from new Mini panels. All panel work is steel. Paint, Ford Vermilion Red.

The GT40 Mini

XVB 816V

One of the maddest Minis ever is Ray Christopher's pickup, which has a Ford GT40 racing engine in the back. Ray used to run a kit car company called GTD, which made very good replicas of the Ford GT40. These were so successful that his life became deeply dull, and he found himself spending way too much time stuck in an office shuffling bits of paper and sorting out production trivia.

His response was to build this Mini. It has caused as much trouble as it has hilarity, and Ray has been banned from every race series he's ever managed to get it entered in. The reason for the multiple bans is simply that the thing is genuinely dangerous. It has a short chassis, the aerodynamics are crap, and as Ray says, you're always steering into a skid: if it gets more than 20° out of line it's going to spin off into the kitty litter. It's like steering a block of flats, he says, because it leans as well as drifting. The power is the same as a GT40, but while the GT40's gorgeous curves serve to keep it stable and smooth at high speeds, the Mini's half-brick aerodynamics have exactly the opposite effect. Despite that, a 1 minute 38 second lap time around Goodwood is respectable, and repeatable as long as the car can be kept pointing mostly forwards.

'Some racing people were saying, you've got to have innovation, got to let him do it: and the others were saying get the loony off the track before he kills himself.' A picture in *Autosport* magazine of the Mini kicking up a 20ft high rooster tail of dirt as it spun off a circuit at full speed did its reputation no good at all.

Banned from the track, Ray took to hillclimbing until the rule books were changed to stop him. '*Que sera*, innit.'

The starting point for this car was a V-reg Mini Traveller with a replica GT40 frame under it, but the rear end of the roof soon came off to be replaced with a pickup bulkhead. That was because driving the car meant you were actually inside the engine bay along with a full-race V8 Ford engine and eight red-hot snake-orgy exhaust pipes: it got a little warm in there. The original Traveller front was also lost in a tyre-wall wipeout early on, but the current van front end has survived for a while. The GT40 Mini has a deep and irresistible attraction for tyre walls, and has snogged them big-time on three occasions so far.

The arches are GRP, but most of the body is still steel and still Mini, although not many of the original car's panels survive. The rear end had to be significantly reconstructed after a substantial crash left a rear wheel sitting on top of the engine.

The chassis is a cut-down replica GT40 frame, with 7in taken out of the sill area. Take it from me, it could use the lost seven inches.

The engine is a period Ford Motorsport 302 (five-litre) with something like 480–500bhp available, more or less what was used in the real GT40s. It's strangled by

← The front end of the Mini contains nothing much, which is one reason why it gets light at 150mph+.

↓ The back end of a pickup offers plenty of room for an engine, and is about the right size for a 302 V8.

↑ The frame of the pickup is an altered GT40 replica chassis.

↑ The only reason the car didn't get its usual huge audience is that the only people present at the track were testing racing cars.

↓ The pickup is MOTable, but not a relaxing motorway cruiser – so it lives in the toy hauler.

the huge silencer needed to drive on obediently shushed British racing circuits – you can make more noise in a library than you can on a British motor racing circuit these days – but even so it packs a fair old punch. The rev limit is now 7,500rpm. It used to be 8,500 but the engine's getting a little tired by now and is worth preserving, rather than risking blowing it up.

Preserving the engine is becoming a moot point these days, though, as Ray has found a new place to race – the Three Hills Challenge on the Isle of Man. Three days of full-on racing, starting at 10:00am and finishing at 4:30pm, after which you go off to the pub with the marshals and the Clerk of the Course. If you want to push your luck and crash into a dry stone dyke you're free to do so, and if you want to make a lot of noise that's OK too.

As Ray says, the car gets lots of attention and lots of smiles from the public and spectators, but not quite so many smiles from drivers and track management if it's spinning down a racetrack among a bunch of expensive racing cars.

As mad Minis go, it's up there.

A lap of Goodwood

A cruise around the Goodwood circuit with Ray in the driving seat starts off with a blast of aural thunder and a brutal kick from behind as the clutch is dumped, then up to 75mph for the first corner. By Frith we're up to 130, and approaching No-Name it's 150–160 on the way in and 105 through the corner. St Mary is slow and difficult, with Ray working the wheel and pushing as hard as he dares – the car is getting very twitchy.

Lavant has new tarmac and sod-all grip, so all four tyres are screaming all the way round. The straight is taken at 170mph, and Ray bawls over the hammering, howling engine, 'THE FRONT GETS A BIT SQUIRLY OVER 160.' I already know that, thanks, I can feel it.

The speedo's not connected because the needle just flaps about at speeds over 150mph, but the car's in top gear and the tacho needle's on the red line so it's not hanging about. More stomping on the brakes, the nose thumps down and you bang through the next lot of corners at around 100mph. You can smell the brakes frying as the speed is clawed down for the last corner and the chicane, and a violent wriggle gets us past that and past the pits in a blur.

I didn't get many laps in, as somebody else trying out the car got more than the critical 20° out of line and flat-spotted all the tyres in a huge cloud of burnt blue rubber smoke before he went off the circuit into the cornfield. He's probably still picking bits of stalk out of his ears.

Tech

ENGINE – Ford Motorsport 302Cl 5-litre V8. Balanced, twin-bolted mains, big valve Motorsport heads, roller rockers. Holley 750 double pumper on Edelbrock manifold, MSD ignition, custom headers and exhaust. Oil cooler, Facet fuel pump.

TRANSMISSION – Four-blade paddle clutch, Renault 30 gearbox and transaxle.

BRAKES – Ford Scorpio standard brake system with twin servos ('almost adequate').

SUSPENSION – Experimental alloy GTD GT40 hubs, Spax adjustable race coilover shocks, 320lb front, 450lb rear. Double wishbones front, four trailing radius rods rear with reverse bottom link and single top arm.

WHEELS AND TYRES – GTD GT40 alloys, 15 x 6J front with P215/60 BF Goodrich Comp T/A, 15 x 10J rear with P265/50 BFG.

BODY and chassis – Modified GTD40 tubular steel chassis, mostly steel body from Mini Traveller. Fuel tanks in sills, piping passes through central floor tunnel. Door hinges from a Peterbilt truck.

INTERIOR – Unidentified but comfy race seats sourced from Beaulieu Autojumble. Luke harnesses. GT40 pedals. Clocks: tacho, speedo, fuel, volts, oil pressure, coolant temp.

International Rescue

John Goolevitch isn't so much mad as just extremely stubborn. Like most members of the Vancouver Mini Club, John paid around $6,000 for this Mini: that's what it costs for a drivable example in North America. He bought it from the Bolivian Consulate in Vancouver, so it had diplomatic plates. He didn't get to keep them, which was a shame – they'd have been useful for sidestepping parking and speeding fines. 'Scusi, Senor Policia – I are deeplomat, no spik English very bueno.'

The car had been a Valentine's Day present to John's wife Jacquie, but she never got near it. She also lost her husband to the garage for a year and a half, but from her point of view she knew where he was and what he was doing, so he says she didn't mind too much.

The Mini had a few rust bubbles here and there but didn't look too bad. He realised that there were some issues, as the Californians say, during a club outing to Oregon in heavy rain, when his feet began to get wet as he drove along. When the convoy stopped, John's carpets were floating in two inches of water, and little waterfalls were pouring out of the sills. His club colleagues, with rather British-style sympathy, bought him a yellow rubber ducky to use as a water depth gauge inside the car. At this point he realised he might be in trouble.

Sure enough, each rust bubble that was poked with a screwdriver turned into a gaping hole, and the sills literally came off in his hands when he started pulling at them. The front end of the car came away more or less in one piece, and not because it was a flip front. The A-panels and front wings disintegrated, revealing that the ends of the dashboard were no longer solidly connected to anything and had been held in place largely by the windscreen and what was left of the scuttle.

The floors mostly disintegrated when kicked, and so did the back seat platform. The transverse seat support panels weren't too bad, but the rusty seat runner securing nuts snapped off rather than coming undone, so that whole area was cut out as well. When all the rust was finally cut back to clean metal, John was left with a solid roof, good roof pillars, some solid areas of floor and most of the rear wings.

In the UK, the car would have been scrapped when the front end fell off. In Canada, the situation is different and the options less palatable. John had lost the significant amount of dollars he had put into buying the car and would have to find the same amount again to buy another usable Mini just to get back to square one, so he decided to build a mostly new Mini shell from repair panels. It would cost plenty, but at least that way he would definitely finish up with a really good rust-free Mini.

He managed to borrow a huge 10,000amp spot welder, which would enable him to restore the Mini not just to new condition, but to concours condition with the right sort and number of spot welds. Mind you, the number of spot welds to be found in a Mini depends on the day of the week on which it was built: Friday cars generally have fewer and more randomly placed welds.

One piece of advice that John would offer to anybody

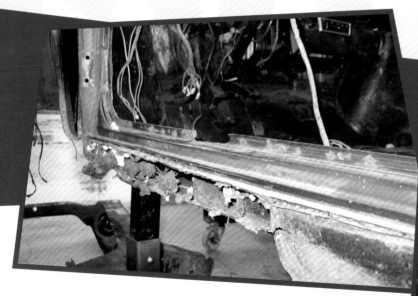

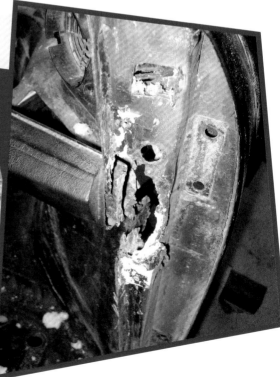

8

← John Goolevitch's Mini finished up much better than new and has won prizes.

↑ Sills? What sills?

→ The doors are hinged further out than this gaping hole, or they would literally have fallen off.

← The body is inverted, the boot lid, panels and floor are gone, so we should be seeing some solid metal…

↑ …but the floorpans are also deeply nasty. That alone would have been terminal for most UK Minis.

tackling a major Mini restoration is to consider replacing major panels rather than repair-patching and reassembling them. He also says that you don't need an expensive welder and can get by just as well with a cheap one, but in the absence of talent and experience I tend to disagree: I have a new, small, cheap MIG welder which is barely able to cope, and I recently got a bigger, older and more serious welder, and with the bigger one welding is much

easier. There's no need to go mad, but buying something in the middle of the amateur welding market is worthwhile, to my mind. John's first go at welding was plating over the speaker hole on the back shelf in this Mini, a good place to start because it's invisible. Success with that encouraged him to carry on.

Having recommended buying whole replacement panels, in John's case financial acuity dictated that anything that could be correctly made from folded and welded sheet metal would be created from scratch, to keep the expensively-imported parts bill down to just massive rather than truly gargantuan. Buying cleverly can be productive, too: the whole rear end of a Mini, from the valance to the window, only cost $80 more than the repair panels needed to restore the original one – and all he had to do was spot-weld the whole assembly on to the main shell. Alignment, he says, wasn't a problem, partly because Minis are small. It's uncharitable but true to point out that they weren't always put together with much precision anyway, particularly if another British Leyland strike was brewing. Or if it was a Friday. Or a Monday.

Sandblasting has pros and cons. John's sandblasting cabinet, he says, is the best tool he ever bought. Conversely, having large thin flat panels sandblasted is a bad idea – they warp unless approached from a shallow angle, gently and patiently and with a less aggressive medium than grit. Classic American cars tend to be made of much thicker steel than British cars, so American shotblasters are used to blasting away with cheery brutality and suffering few disastrous consequences.

Tech

ENGINE – 1,293cc, .020 oversize bores/pistons, Pertronix ignition module, LCB manifold, RC40 exhaust, otherwise standard. Original engine was 998cc.

TRANSMISSION – Heavy-duty clutch, otherwise standard four-speed all-synchro.

SUSPENSION – Standard dry rubber cones.

BRAKES – Non-assisted, drums all round.

WHEELS AND TYRES – Standard restored 3.5J x 10 steel rims, Kumho 145 x 10in tyres.

INTERIOR – Just Stitching Around piped seats, Newton Commercial carpets with extra binding.

EXTERIOR – 1972 Mini 1000 to Canadian spec, extensively restored and repainted in Black Tulip. British spec sidelight/indicators and bumpers fitted.

The doors on John's car looked OK, but he stuffed a small camera inside them and took some flash pictures – then having seen the resulting images he pulled the old skins off the doors and replaced them, fortunately quite an easy and cheap task and a much better idea than repairing them. I've tried both, and reskinning takes about 10% of the effort and time of repairing rusty door panels.

The whole underside of the car has been coated in Gravel-Guard, a thick and permanent coating. The topside got ten coats of hand-rubbed primer before the shiny paint went on, but you can probably see that by looking at the pictures.

The rest of the components of the car looked quite nice because they were generally still in good condition – it had just been the rust problem that was severe. The wiring was dismantled, cleaned, wire-brushed and gently media-blasted where appropriate, then rewrapped and clipped back in. A new headlining was fitted – a pain-in-the-bum job every time. The brake and clutch cylinders were cleaned, blasted, re-rubbered and clear-coated, then refitted. The 998cc engine was replaced with a bored-out (to 1293cc) 1275. Another tip from John, on reassembling a restored and painted car – it's safer to drop the car on to the engine rather than to jack the engine up into the car – there's less risk of scratching brand new paint.

The Black Tulip paint in question, a deep purple, very '70s and quite cool, had originally been matched with orange nylon velour seats – also very '70s but hideously uncool. Part of John wanted to refit the concours-correct seats, but when he put the rear seat back in the car he had to take it straight out again – the colour was just too upsetting. The seats were stripped, re-foamed and re-trimmed in black with purple piping.

The overall cost was pretty brutal. Remember that in Canada, Minis are expensive foreign exotica, and so are the spares – a new front wing that can be bought for 20 quid cash at a UK car show, or a tenner if you wait until they're loading their van at the end of the show, costs $90 (£50) by the time it gets to John's door, and a front apron is $120 (£66).

The total cost? 'I didn't want to keep track, because it would be too depressing,' he says, 'so I don't really know.' But we all know roughly what a full restoration costs, so why do it in the first place, rather than just throw the scrap Mini car away and buy a good one?

'Because it was *my* Mini.'

Fair enough.

↑↑ After a year and a half of hard work with spot welder and rubbing block, John is a happy bunny.

↑ Purple piping on black seats looks nice – the original orange nylon was in the end just too indigestible.

The Miniha

⬇ Robin has chosen to go for a stock look, largely because he wanted the car to be a sleeper. It's more fun humiliating a Porsche if it looks like you're driving a fairly ordinary Mini.

TUA 968W

Robin Knapton is well pleased with his Yamaha R1-powered Mini. When he began the project the R1 was the fastest bike in the world, so that's a pretty good starting point for a powerplant for a bike-engined Mini. The R1 motor has a reputation for being indestructible, and it's also less expensive than a Hayabusa engine. It may not have the torque of the bigger Hayabusa engine, but 285bhp/ton and 4.5 seconds to 60mph is quite frisky.

With the engine and the drive at the back, all the power goes into forward motion rather than rubber smoke: the car is extremely fast. It's still a real steel Mini, though – or to be more accurate, what remains of the Mini's shell is still steel. It's a Z-Cars conversion, but it's not one of their full-on terror machines, which are a bike engine in a roll cage with a plastic Mini-shaped hat on it.

As a Mini enthusiast and a superbike enthusiast, Robin successfully combined both in one vehicle. He likes the way the engine will rev to double the rpm of a Mini engine, and he likes the way it spins its wheels on take-off but still has plenty left when you plant it, whatever speed you happen to be going. He also enjoys humiliating Porsche 911 Carrera Turbos: he can take them, no bother, up to 120mph. After which he can legitimately back off anyway, as the job is done.

One of the other things he really likes about this car is the visceral excitement it generates, even at legal speeds. He's owned Subarus and big bikes aplenty, but any serious throttle action lasting more than five seconds on either of those could cost him his licence. The Miniha, on the other hand, feels about 100mph faster than it actually is. The engine doesn't just start like boring old production cars: it explodes into life, and then it sits there growling urgently, twitching and nervy, gagging to go, like a greyhound in its trap. Robin just sits there waiting for it to warm up, as the engine trembles and twitches in its kennel behind you.

When he lets it out of the trap, the noise is appalling. At 9,000rpm you're thinking for God's sake please change gear before it throws a rod, but that's when the cam comes in and it really gets going: the rev limiter cuts in at 14,200rpm. By the end of second gear, the scenery is a blur, the entire universe has gone screaming mad, your head is having trouble staying on, every muscle is rigid, and the speedo reads… 60mph.

Oo-er. Felt like 150mph. *Click click click* up the gearbox, and the engine is now producing a loud tenor rumble as we cruise to an empty road to give it some proper exercise. There's no rubber cush drive as there is in the bike's rear hub, so there's lots of clacking and banging through the transmission, amplified by the biscuit-tin acoustics of the bare Mini shell.

The suspension settings are pretty hard-core, and ride comfort is not helped by the cast-iron A-series anchor in the front being entirely missing. The tyres are pumped to 18lb, as the car only weighs around 600 kilos, and the

9

⬇The whole front end is very nicely custom-made in steel from Mini panels.

↑ Digidash avoids the need for any other instruments, and also avoids Yamaha/BL sensor-to-instrument clashes. It runs through its functions and settles on road-speed display as its usual default function.

↑ Even with no engine it always seems to be crowded in a Mini's engine bay. Fuel tank, brake servo and radiator are at the front.

↑ The engine bay looks almost empty: the tiny engine is tucked away at the front. The rear suspension offers adjustable coilovers, an anti-roll bar and disc brakes.

↑ The chain drive connects to a custom differential provided by Z-Cars.

already stiff Mini ride is stiffened yet further by the weight reduction. If you imagine being towed along a rough road in an engineless Mini by a jet fighter, that's more or less what this thing feels like.

With a stretch of clear road ahead, Robin punches it properly, and when the tyres get a grip, it goes scream SCREAM clack, scream SCREAM clack, much like before, but after the sixth click it's time to back off as all the needles have swivelled a very long way past sensible. The second big scream is caused by the cams coming on: the power smacks in with such a bang that I can't imagine you would be able to stay on top of a Yamaha R1 bike at full throttle in the lowest gears. It must feel like being rear-ended by a dump truck when the cams hit on an R1 bike. In a steel Mini, though, you can actually use the full power in all gears, and of course being a Mini it can corner much, much harder than a bike. I reckon this Miniha would cream an R1 on a racetrack, even if the rider had *cojones* the size of grapefruit.

After a short while this level of noise gets pretty tiresome, and Robin keeps a pair of earplugs in the ashtray for going home after a blast. There's no soundproofing at all, and the engine bulkhead, an inch behind your shoulder, is a single sheet of aluminium. If you wanted to civilise a Miniha with sound deadening and carpets, you could – but I don't know that you would necessarily want to. At full welly the exhaust screams like a dozen electrocuted sopranos, and the crackling, spitting and popping of half-burnt fuel on the overrun sounds like a gaggle of Type 35 Bugattis cornering at the Le Mans Classic.

→ → This is the view of the car that most people see as it screams past them. There are clues as to why – the exhaust, the side-window air intakes, the yammering scream from the exhaust.

The stance with the low back end isn't a styling choice: Z-Cars have found that lowering the rear end to this height achieves the best handling.

Getting the car to this point was… easy is the wrong word, as it's a big project, but it was straightforward and fun. The Mini was stripped to the shell, the rust was repaired with new panels, the rear end was chopped out and it was painted ready for the Z-Cars kit. Robin rates Z-Cars highly. He bought the kit and also the engine from them, guaranteed to be a good runner for £1,600, and fitted the kit to the car with no problems at all.

The kit starts with a roll hoop in the usual position behind your head, from which the suspension and engine are suspended. There are new trailing arms with disc brakes, and driveshafts lead inwards from the hubs to a chain sprocket and a Z-Cars differential. You can add an electric reverse gear, or get out and push, whichever. Oddly enough, while a reverse gear is not currently required for road cars it's compulsory for racing. If you finish up stranded on the apex of a corner after a misjudgement and a spin, there may not be room to get out of the way of approaching competitors by going forwards. The Z-cars electric reverse system is basically a converted starter motor, but it's £400 and Robin decided to skip it.

There's an anti-roll bar and a set of light alloy coilover shocks, and most of the joints are rose-jointed and adjustable. The engine sits as far forward as it will go in order to achieve the best possible mid-rear-engine weight distribution – you could almost bang it with your elbow – and the six gears are sequential. The gear lever simply clicks forward six times to get into top. You don't really use the clutch going up the gearbox, just lift off the throttle a little,

although it's kinder to the engine and box to blip and declutch on the way down.

At the front, there's a crash bar that's attached to the rollcage, to the Mini subframe, and to the body, and there are brackets for the adjustable front lightweight coilover shocks, the radiator, and the racing fuel cell. The suspension is adjustable, and the brakes are Mini four-pot discs.

Many people choose a plakky flip front, but Robin welded together a top-class steel one. Somehow steel flip fronts always look just a little sharper, a little better: they're worth the effort, considerable though it is.

Six months of happily busy weekends saw the rest of the car's assembly and the plumbing and electrics going in, and quite quickly the big day came when the engine was fired up for the first time. On its first drive there was a nasty vibration, for which Robin couldn't find a reason or cure. Z-Cars took the car in and sorted it out over the next couple of weeks, free of charge, and gave it back driving perfectly.

Since then Robin has sorted out better cold air flow to the carbs, and has changed the glass rear side-windows for drilled Perspex ones with a custom air scoop that helps to feed cold air to the carbs and to keep the engine cool. He's also devoted a lot of dedicated effort to learning to get the best out of an evilly fast rear-wheel-drive Mini while retaining his driving licence.

If you ever see this car for sale, buy it: there won't be anything wrong with it, but Robin has the Need for Speed, and he's seen Z-Cars' rollcage-framed GRP Monte Carlo which is even faster than this one.

ENGINE – Yamaha R1, 2002: 998cc, four-cylinder transverse liquid-cooled EFI DOHC 20-valve 170bhp aluminium bike engine. Pipercross air filter, NGK Laser iridium spark plugs, Z-Cars wiring loom. Bosch universal fuel pump. Custom-tuned exhaust. 1970s Fiat Uno radiator, Kenlowe 12in fan.

TRANSMISSION – Multi-plate clutch, six-speed sequential integral gearbox, Z-Cars custom chain drive and diff. Reverse gear operated by manual owner-limb contra-progression, ie get out and push.

BRAKES – Servo-assisted Mini pedal and master cylinder, braided lines throughout. Front, MiniSport four-pot calipers, solid Mini discs. Rear, Ford discs and calipers. Custom handbrake.

SUSPENSION – Front, adjustable tie bars and control arms, coilovers. Rear, independent axle, fixed chain drive and diff, halfshafts, trailing arms, coilovers, rose-jointed adjustable anti-roll bar. Pro Tech alloy coilover shock absorbers all round, adjustable for compression and rebound.

WHEELS AND TYRES – 7J x 13 Minilite alloys, with 175/50 x 13 Yokohama A539 tyres, set at 18psi.

EXTERIOR – 1981 Mini shell, Sport Pack arches, MkI grille surround, custom seamless steel flip front, Perspex rear windows with air scoops to cool engine, Ford Rosso Red paint.

INTERIOR – Monaco Sport bucket seats, three-point Sabelt harnesses, Z-Cars full rollcage, EVO Digidash.

PERFORMANCE – 0–60: 4.5 seconds. BHP per ton: 275. Top speed: 120mph so far. Fuel economy: 25–30mpg.

Moking

Many North American Mini Mokes are used for autocrossing, which is local-level, budget motorsport that anybody can enjoy. Most American Mini meetings feature an autocross – all you need is a car park and some cones.

Minis, of course, are brilliant at autocrossing. They're short, with a wheel at each corner, they have firm suspension and they handle well. They also allow even a novice to make excitingly rapid progress because front-wheel drive is quite amateur-friendly: the front wheels tend to drag you in the right direction even if they're skidding a bit. Push your luck as a normal driver in a rear-drive car and you'll usually spin out very quickly.

Minis are top autocross tools, then. So imagine a Mini with a longer wheelbase for extra stability, with the heavy roof, glasshouse and doors removed, with a strong engine and a stiff boxed perimeter chassis – it would be the perfect autocrosser.

That's exactly what a Mini Moke is.

For its original purpose, as a military jeep, it was comically useless. The cunning plan was that Mokes would be stacked in a Hercules transport aircraft with parachutes attached, and would then be thrown out to land on the battlefield, where troops would jump into them and drive off to kill people. The stacking idea worked brilliantly – with the windscreens down, the flat mudguards of the bottom Moke are ideally placed for the wheels of the Moke on top.

The fatal flaw was the total lack of ground clearance. If the parachuted Moke happened to land on a road, no worries, jump in and drive off. If it landed on a flat dry field with a convenient gate leading on to a road, you might get away with that as well if it wasn't too bumpy. If it was raining, forget it: if one wheel spun in the mud, the Moke would go nowhere. Even military purchasing authorities spotted this flaw, and they formed an orderly queue not to buy Mokes. The only people who did buy them were hippies, and latterly Caribbean hotels.

That lack of ground clearance made the Moke one of the most useless military vehicles ever, but the same

← The author spent a cheerful few days driving this restored standard 850cc Moke around Tennessee in 100° heat, and enjoyed every moment: you don't need air-conditioning in a Moke.

↓ The interior of a Moke is a fairly Spartan environment. This one has a 118bhp engine and many more clocks than the standard lonely speedo.

→ Most Mokers stick with the traditional A-series Mini engine, but one can't help wondering about a Honda Vtec. You wouldn't even need to alter the bodywork…

10

Vancouver Mini Club's Rob Fram shows how it's done. Strong engine, sticky tyres, throw the back end out just enough and use the power to haul the Moke around the cones. A fair amount of blue smoke from tailpipe and tyres, but a tidy run with no squished cones.

low ground clearance, combined with its lack of a roof and windows, gave it a centre of gravity lower than the ethical standards of a cabinet minister. For something to throw around a small car park, at max speed, slaloming between cones, you really can't get anything better. Even if you designed a pure autocross racer it would finish up looking like a Mini Moke.

The other bonus of the Moke is that you can provide excellent entertainment for yourself, a few friends and the general public simply by driving one around the streets, and you get to join the Mini world, which is full of amusing, eccentric, friendly and helpful people who energetically organise themselves to have all sorts of harmless fun.

Mokes have even been credited with curing shyness: a Moker friend used to suffer from painful shyness until he bought a Moke, after which people wouldn't leave him alone, so he had no choice but to become gregarious and friendly.

Mokes everywhere get a huge amount of attention, but the questions in America are always the same. You can have fun making up new answers to the same old questions, though.

Is it legal? (No, I made the licence plates myself.)

Is it electric? (Have a listen to the engine noise and take a wild guess.)

Is it a golf cart? (No, I'm way too young to play golf.)

What does it do to the gallon? (About four times as much as yours.)

Can I see your licence and registration, please? (Um, no problem, officer. I do apologise if I was mistakenly going a bit fast back there, this is a 1966 Moke and the speedo's not very accurate.)

The Rotary Club

Rotary

↓ GRP flip front is absolutely clean and devoid of any clutter. It also has a subtle downward slope to it.

Jeff Griffin has used a race-derived spaceframe chassis, a Mazda rotary engine, rear-wheel drive and a custom plastic front in his Mini, but for all that it's still a Mini.

It was a guy called Kool-Aid who started the project a good few years back. Kool-Aid is a fizzy American powdered sugar drink, but it's also Kool-Aid's nickname, and a top nickname it is too.

The chassis was based on the design concept of a successful racing GT5 Mini built by veteran racing car driver and designer Joe Huffaker, who was to American Minis what John Cooper was to British Minis. Joe won three SCCA Championships in his Mini from 2000 to 2002. He started with a racing Healey in 1954, and went on to build racing versions of MGBs, Jaguars, Healeys, Austin-Healeys and Jensen-Healeys, and then moved on to Minis later as the competition possibilities offered by the Mini format became clear. So the Huffaker-inspired chassis made by Kool-Aid was authentic Mini history, although it wasn't British Mini history.

Joe Huffaker is still making old British cars go faster, and still sells stonking dry-sumped race engines for Spridgets, which of course almost fit Minis… check out www.huffakerengineering.com.

This particular Mini was a massively ambitious project, and Kool-Aid gradually came to a stop as he realised he was never going to finish it. Having made his very major contribution, he passed the project on to his friend Jeff Griffin, who managed to make quite reasonable progress over the next four years. However, an increasingly successful kitchen cabinet business

began to interfere more and more with building the car, and Jeff's progress also ground to a halt. However, during his four years of patient but stop-start development, Jeff had figured out exactly what needed to be done to finish the car, and how. He couldn't do it himself any more, but he could now afford to have somebody else do it on his behalf. Fortunately, Jeff's home town of Charlotte, North Carolina, is an excellent place to be inventing new cars, as there are numerous racing shops around to serve the local NASCAR and SCCA racing scene. Racing engineer Todd Hayworth was entrusted with the task of carrying on where Jeff had left off.

The car was actually quite well on the way by that point: the rollcage and internal body bracing had been constructed, and the roof had also been chopped. The roof chop is interesting – the height of the roof has been cut by an inch and a half, but the windscreen remains the standard size, although made of Lexan rather than glass. Jeff cut up the entire A-pillar and scuttle assembly, moved the bottom of the screen forwards and pulled the top of the screen backwards, and refitted the original screen surround so that a standard screen could still be used – an excellent trick for anybody considering a relatively subtle roof job on a Mini. It's not a big chop compared to Jason Neumann's four-inch roof amputation in Chapter 2, but Jeff's roofline still looks just that bit cooler, reduces

◤ Rear-wheel-drive Minis offer very useful rearward weight transfer, so rather than spinning the front wheels they just grab and go.

↑ The entire car displays clear thinking, ergonomic design and neat execution. Big rad ensures no cooling probs.

↗ The engine is small and mounted right back, so the engine bay is tidy, neat and uncrowded. Carb, alternator and triple Tilton hydraulic cylinders all look very much at home in there.

→ Enormous double-pumper Holley has four huge chokes to feed three sort-of cylinders. It doesn't flood the engine, just makes it go faster.

aerodynamic drag just that extra bit, and rakes the windscreen back just a few degrees – all of which makes a worthwhile contribution to gaining a few extra seconds on a racetrack lap. The car may finish up just a track toy rather than in actual competition, but that's not the point – if it's a race car let's get it right.

In this case there's no point in getting aerated about the chopping-up of an original MkI Mini, because all that existed of the Mini in question was a percentage of a shell, and it was in nasty condition to boot. There wasn't even enough of the car left to establish what year it was, although it had external hinge holes and inner door frame structures confirming that it had been a MkI. The worthwhile bits of the old Mini were dutifully recycled into the new monster, although to be honest not much was left in usable condition: the roof and quite a lot of the rear exterior panelling is still original, but that's about all. The wheel arches are by Fortech, altered and blended in.

The doors look like Mini doors, but they're actually handmade from sheet steel with tubular frames, constructed from scratch. The one-piece and one-off detachable flip front carries Mini lights and grille, but it's been reshaped to droop downwards for better aerodynamics: this was possible because the Mazda engine

is a small barrel-shaped device mounted approximately beneath the windscreen and scuttle, and it doesn't require the high bonnet line that's dictated for most Minis by the height of the tall, long-stroke A-series engine that also has a gearbox beneath it. The less frontal area your car has, the faster you go – so the raked-back screen and droopy front all help.

The lack of windscreen wipers, an impractical idea in Britain, is usually not a problem in Jeff's locale: Georgia and North and South Carolina in 2008 were experiencing a long and serious drought, which naturally broke for the day to allow enough rain to make a Brit feel very much at home, shooting a car with drips going down his neck and not enough light. The drought then came back the next day and carried on afterwards. Normally most days are dry, so a fun car with no wipers makes sense out there.

Getting a longitudinally-mounted engine, gearbox, axle and Jeff all jammed inside a lowered Mini shell took some doing, and involved much sitting, shifting things, sitting again, shifting things, and in the end a custom gear linkage was still required to put the gearknob within comfortable reach: the gear lever had to end up somewhere fairly natural, because awkward gearchanges make for slow gearchanges. The gearbox didn't have to be a cool piece of

sculpture hand-carved from turned aluminium billet, though – making it that way was just more fun. All the work ethic, perfectionism and money that went into getting the gear lever right did not continue when it came to the steering wheel: it came from a go-kart, cost all of ten bucks and plopped straight on. Tell you what, it looks and works just fine too.

Something that's not usually used by longitudinal Mini artists is the Mini-based idea of using the radiator sideways on, beside the engine if room is tight – the automatic tendency is to put it in front where it looks right. A big enough side-mounted rad, properly ducted and fanned, can work as well as it does in a Mini. Jeff's front-mounted radiator arrangement works just fine and looks nice too, so no worries. The fan rarely turns itself on if the car is moving, which is the most reliable indication that the system is working well.

The Mazda rotary is a hot-running little engine, even if the cooling system and the internal engine temperatures are correct. One of Jeff's future tasks is to get the cabin heat down a little, as it gets a bit tropical in there when the engine gets up to its full working temperature.

Would he use another rotary engine in a Mini? Having tried this one out, he probably wouldn't. It's hot, it's frenetic, it guzzles fuel, but the worst thing about it is the noise. Rotaries rev high, and they make a nasty and ear-splitting noise. There isn't room for any more silencers under the car, and the existing pair of silencers, although

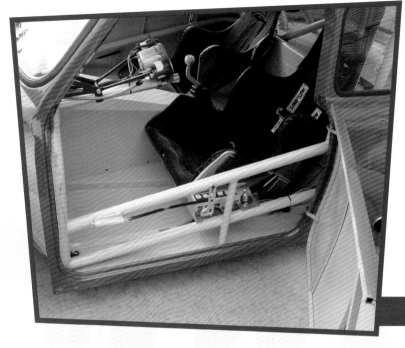

they're proper silencers rather than straight-through Cherry Bombs or whatever, simply can't shut much of the noise down. Jeff was quite relieved when the photo shoot was over, as he had just moved into a new house and didn't want to annoy his brand-new neighbours too much by wasping noisily up and down the road.

On the track the rotary would be great, screaming its nuts off and generating even more adrenaline, but on the

↑ Stonking door bars are comforting, particularly when the doors themselves are just skin and tubing.

← The licence plate identifies the car as from North Carolina on the USA's East Coast, halfway between New York and Florida,

track you're focused on pushing it as hard as you can, hopefully just short of pushing it 1% too hard, and you're also wearing a crash helmet which would cut some noise. On the road the raspy buzz would soon become a pain.

Rotary engines are also smelly and have emissions issues – they have to burn some oil, like a two-stroke, for internal lubrication of the rotor tips. The principle of their operation is that a spinning triangular rotor rotates inside the oval tubular engine casing (it's epitrochoidal, to be exact, if you want to be flash) and creates three spaces that act as combustion chambers. There are no camshafts and no pistons or rods, so there's a limit to what you can do to a rotary engine to make it more amusing. Spiky cams and balanced rods and pistons are not options, as there are none of any of them. All you can really do to a rotary is to get the porting perfect and then try to jam as much air and fuel mixture into the engine as possible.

There's a fan-base for Mazda's rotary sports cars who enjoy playing with these engines: they frequently achieve more power by turbocharging, and sometimes by twin-turbocharging and by nitrous injection, but in Jeff's case the engine is topped by a cavernous normally-aspirated Holley double-pumper four-barrel carb that lets in a massive 650cu ft a minute. It's intended for something like a five-to-seven-litre V8 and is about four times the size of a Mini carb. The Mazda rotary engine displaces 1.3 litres, although that number doesn't mean much unless it's applied to a piston engine. The Mazda engine in the Mini is still standard apart from the carb and some porting, and from experience Jeff is expecting something over 225bhp when the car is dynoed. For a 1,450lb car, 225bhp is going to be quite nippy.

I suspect that a bike engine would do the same job better, although it's not cheap to get 225bhp out of a bike engine. I wouldn't be surprised to find either a Hayabusa engine or a violently modified MX5 or Honda 2000 engine in the car next time I pass through North Carolina.

The rest of the car's drivetrain is thoroughly sorted. Rear-wheel drive for a fun performance car is obviously way better than front-wheel, and the Mazda in-line gearbox is strong and quite light with slick, quick gearchanges. It's an RX7 casing with MX5 gears, which have closer ratios than those of the larger RX7.

The rear axle is also Mazda, and has a very useful 'posi' limited-slip diff.

The suspension and steering are really race-derived, largely because of the availability of good racing gear within easy reach. Bilstein have a location 20 miles away, so Jeff's shocks were made by them to his specification. The steering rack is from a Legends racer, and was designed into the front suspension way back. The front suspension is double wishbone with a monster aluminium anti-roll bar

↑↑ The Bilstein shocks aren't adjustable, but were custom-built to Jeff's spec for the car.

↑ The hefty anti-roll bar runs through the main front chassis beam: very elegant design and engineering.

↓ In order to get the turned billet gear lever in the right place, the driver has to sit in the back seat.

that attaches to the very front of the chassis.

The rear end is controlled by a four-bar set-up, which inevitably has short bars because of the shortness of the car. The two lower trailing arms are set at 45° rather like a Lotus Cortina, and also, anachronistically, like my 1958 Chevy Delray. These allow vertical movement but restrict lateral movement. The upper trailing arms just go straight backwards, keeping the axle vertical. As a system it's not ideal, but given the space available there weren't many options. Using something close to the original Mini suspension combined with rear-wheel drive would be ideal, but it would be very complicated and would require castings and special hubs. In any case, this is a fast street and track car with very limited suspension travel, so any changes in axle geometry due to short suspension arms wouldn't be a big deal anyway. Anything Mini-shaped with stiff suspension is going to have pretty impressive handling in any case, certainly when you put it up against anything else of its type that it's likely to meet on an American racetrack.

So – another top mad Mini. The engine hasn't in the end turned out to be ideal, but every aspect of the rest of the car is spot on, and Jeff has plenty of time to play with it and consider potential powerplant improvements as time goes on.

ENGINE – Mazda 13b 1,300cc rotary, with fast road porting and a 650CFM Holley double-pumper four-choke carb. Custom aluminium radiator, custom rear-mounted oil cooler, dual silencers, expected bhp +/–225.

TRANSMISSION – In-line Mazda RX7 gearbox casing with close-ratio Mazda MX5 gear cluster, propshaft to narrowed RX7 rear axle with 4.11:1 limited-slip Positraction diff.

SUSPENSION – Front, double wishbone with ¾in alloy anti-roll bar, Bilstein custom-valved shocks with 250lb springs. Rear, 45° lower trailing arms provide lateral and longitudinal location, straight upper trailing arms provide longitudinal location; Bilstein custom-valved shocks with 200lb springs. Steering rack from Legends race car.

BRAKES – Wilwood four-pot aluminium calipers all round, adjustable balance.

WHEELS AND TYRES – Panasport 7J x 13 wheels with 215/50 x 13 Sumitomo tyres.

EXTERIOR – Floorpan and chassis resembles a Joe Huffaker racing Mini design extended by 2in. Cage is Jeff's own: body is partly MkI steel Mini with a 1.5in roof chop and partly GRP replica with Fortech arches and modified nose. 1,450lb all-up weight. House of Kolor pearl orange paint.

INTERIOR – ATL ten-gallon fuel cell. Race seats, Simpson harnesses, $10 go-kart steering wheel, Auto Meter tacho, oil pressure, water temperature, voltmeter, fuel pressure, speedo. Lexan windows.

⬇ The stance and ground clearance of this Mini is spot on. It looks mean and moody but doesn't scrape its bodywork as much as you would expect.

Offroad

↑ Functional rather than elegant – the box on the front bodywork is where your foot goes.

← When driving in the rough, the road wheels are changed for the offroad ones: the spare wheels and tyres add weight over the driving wheels.

→ The white Mountaineer is a development of the earlier Mosquito in the background, resplendent in attention-grabbing pink. Hollier apparently has no worries about his masculinity.

The Mini Moke wasn't an auspicious start for Minis and offroading, but one or two people have made the Mini concept work quite well in the kak.

As we've established elsewhere in this compendium (Chapter 10), Mini Mokes, although cool and top fun, are crap unless they're on smooth tarmac. However, there have been a few successful offroad Minis. Two in particular are worthy of a mention, one because it was actually rather effective, and the other because although it was as good an offroader as it's possible to construct with a compromised FWD-only Mini drivetrain, it was adopted by a particular collection of loonies who got more fun out of it than anybody is really entitled to.

The very competent Mini-based offroader was designed and built by Chris Hollier, already mentioned earlier in this very book (Chapter 5), and it was called the Mountaineer. It was a development of his Mosquito, and both that and the Mountaineer were basically rollcages with a wheel at each corner and initially a Mini engine and box in the back. The pink Mosquito in the background had a tiny but loyal band of enthusiasts, but it was still really a slightly mad road car rather than an offroader. The Mountaineer was definitely an offroader, sold in small numbers for competition, and was a much more serious bit of kit.

With the engine and everything else at the back, all the weight was on the driven wheels, so traction was excellent, and the rack on the back was designed to carry the spare tyres. The idea was that you would drive on road tyres to your chosen patch of mud or offroading event, change them over for tractorish offroad tyres with about 20psi of air in them, and then strap the road tyres on top to add weight over the back wheels. The overall weight was low, and as it happens four-wheel drive is not the most important feature of successful offroaders – shortness, high ground clearance and low overhangs are more important, and 4WD is only really crucial for wading though deep goop where you're more or less swimming. I've been amazed at how far a 2WD Cortina-based kit jeep would go on a purpose-built offroad track.

The Mountaineer was a top tool for offroad racing, but sadly not many people are queuing up to buy vehicles specifically built to do that, so it joined Chris's extensive list of interesting past projects.

12

↑ The Mountaineer is as happy airborne as earthbound, and is built to take hard landings in its stride. The Mini componentry evolved out of it: you need long, soft springs for yumping, because landing on Mini rubber-doughnut suspension takes your fillings out.

→ The Scamp's ground clearance is certainly better than a Moke, but its body design shares the Moke's styling subtlety.

↓ The roof frame is also the rollcage: doors and roof are optional.

The more practical Scamp was a much bigger commercial success, although less agile in the kak. Success in kit car terms means several hundred were made per decade, rather than just… several.

Mini Scamps were built for many years in a collection of rural sheds by the charming Andrew McLean, who lived in a beached boat in a farmyard. He's still making them now, but with Suzuki Jeeps as a base rather than Minis.

The Scamp achieved offroad progress by being indestructible rather than by having top traction and ground clearance. If you only have two-wheel drive, an effective technique is to select second gear, grip the steering wheel firmly (keeping your thumbs clear of the spokes), mash your foot down flat on the throttle, and don't back off until you either get to flat dry ground again or hit something.

Andrew challenged me to give his demo Scamp a proper test on a nearby muddy forest track, suggesting that most visiting journalists were pussies and wouldn't give it any real exercise, so I applied the above technique with enthusiasm. A small tree had fallen down across the path, but it looked small enough to be either pushed out of the way or driven over the top of, so I kept my foot down. Yee-ha. The Scamp seriously impressed me, only losing its number plate and exhaust system along a route that would have given a Range Rover a hard time.

The Scamp Club, at least the members I used to talk to, were barking mad. They genuinely thought it was top fun to roll a Scamp down a mountain, and during their big summer camping get-together their favourite game was field-surfing, which involved towing each other at 40mph on dustbin lids across a wet field behind a Scamp. Most car clubs have amusing little games involving driving slowly and skilfully with fishing rods and rubber ducks, but the Scamp nutters considered that their annual summer camping holiday had been a big success if nobody was seriously injured. Top bunch of chaps, up there with the Dutton club in the stratosphere of kit car eccentricity.

The Scamp itself was fully Mini-based, but many of them had different rear trailing arm arrangements or spacers to allow bigger wheels and chunky tyres. The chassis/frame was made from light welded steel tubing, well braced and very strong, and skinned in aluminium sheeting. There was no wussy nonsense about curves, and the whole approach was utilitarian in the extreme. The back end was a box that you could fill with seats, and the options list was only limited by the builder's imagination. Some roofs and sides were aluminium, some were canvas, some were missing.

Although the standard Scamp is attractive in a functional sort of way, many home-built Scamps are truly hideous, and reflect their owners' idiosyncrasies: some have elevated idiosyncrasy to an art form, and a total lack of artistic talent never stopped any of them. Scamps are available from a few hundred quid, if you think you can handle this level of fun – check out the club's site at www. scampownersclub.co.uk.

↑ With the doors and the roof attached, the Scamp is actually surprisingly weatherproof and mudproof.

→ Andrew McLean suggested I was too wimpy to drive on his offroad test course. Here he is picking up the exhaust pipe I tore off while doing it.

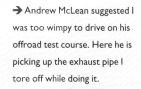

↓ Wheel arches are legally required to cover the wheels, so why waste time and metal doing any more than that?

Street
and
Strip

At first glance it's just a very red and shiny Mini pickup. Hang on a minute, though…

Lynn Schoonover's Mini pickup is mad, but like the best mad ideas it has been carefully and seriously executed, and on closer examination it turned out to be astonishingly competent. It really shouldn't be. If the chassis had been built for proper drag racing it would have been a lot bigger and longer, and jamming the sort of mechanicals and chassis you would expect to see under a street/strip '57 Chevy into a tiny Mini pickup should have compromised it into relative uselessness.

The car is at heart a joke, but it's a beautifully crafted joke with a hell of a punchline. Lynn offered to light up the tyres and burn some rubber for the shoot, because a red pickup emerging from huge clouds of blue rubber smoke would have looked way cool, but Dinkee doesn't do a smoke show, it just takes off like a *Daily Mail* reporter on the scent of a paedophile story. Every time Lynn stamped on his throttle the pickup just hooked up, the rear end squatted down and it took off. It just refused to indulge in any cheap showing off, and was only interested in serious business.

It's actually quite drivable and tractable on the road as well, although not very comfortable as the enormous transmission tunnel takes up most of the cabin, leaving only a few inches on either side for feet and pedals. There are no seats as such, because there isn't room: there's a sort of padded bench and that's about it.

The Fuellie cam in the Chevy engine was originally designed to work with early fuel-injection Corvettes, so it doesn't have a particularly fierce profile. The cam isn't spiky enough to make the engine wobble and splutter at idle, it just gives the V8 a bit of an attitude at tickover and allows more action higher up the tacho.

The reasons for the pickup's astonishing competence start at the back, with a pair of huge Mickey Thompson street-legal slick tyres with treads cut in them, mounted on American Racing wheels which are bolted more or less straight on to the brakes and the diff, which is the traditional extremely strong 9in Ford.

Dragstrip traction requires monster tyres, but street rod style requires that the tyres remain inside the original sides of the car's bodywork. Obviously most of the pickup bed is occupied with the tubs required to cover the tyres, but by deleting most of the rear axle, the tyres are not just inside the arches but quite significantly inside them.

The front tyres are as thin as the rear ones are fat, and they're the same size as those fitted to a Citroën 2CV: compared to the massive rubber on the rear they look like moped tyres. However, they're not just stylistically and functionally correct for drag racing, they also allow lots of room between them to get the 5.7-litre Corvette spec engine and its headers inside the Mini shell. Not much of the engine and box are actually inside the engine bay, but they've all been stuffed inside the shell of the Mini, even leaving room for a radiator at the front, although only just enough room: clearance is in millimetres.

The front has been extended and louvred and reshaped to droop a little, partly for a little extra speed advantage and partly for style. As speeds during the last stages of a dragstrip run are well into treble mph figures, the half-brick aerodynamics of a Mini pickup have a real negative impact on speed during the later part of the quarter-mile, so a smooth droopy front is worth the effort. Fitting louvres in the bonnet right above the exhaust manifolds is also a smart move and helps to

↓The side view reveals something of what's really going on. It's still largely a Mini, but the wheels and the front end don't look right at all.

← From behind, the extent of the changes begins to become clear. This isn't really a Mini at all, it's a psycho dragstrip monster masquerading as a Mini.

↙ 327CI Corvette V8 is neatly tucked under the scuttle. Detailing throughout is to a very high standard.

↓ The extent of the front modifications can be seen here: about 5in has been added to the rear edges of the bonnet and wings.

↑ The flat sheeting of the pickup bed has been replaced with a stonking chassis and a 9in Ford diff, with huge wheels and drag slicks bolted to it. Handling will obviously never be as good as a Mini again, but isn't bad at all.

keep engine bay temperatures a little more reasonable. The radiator and cooling system on the Mini proved very effective on the day of the shoot: it was 105° in Riverside, California, and we were asking the Mini to launch under full power, reverse back up the road for a hundred feet and launch again, maybe twenty times, one after the other. The engine was certainly getting hot, but it wasn't getting bothered, and wasn't throwing the hissy fit to which it was fully entitled after half an hour of that sort of treatment.

The engine is a blueprinted 327 Chevy, originally from a '65 Corvette, bored out plus 30 thou, fairly stock but for Edelbrock aluminium heads, a Corvette Fuellie cam and a fat Carter AFB carb on a Weiand inlet manifold. The headers are obviously custom – there are plenty of Chevy header options and plenty of Mini exhaust manifold options, but off-the-shelf Mini V8 headers are rarer than honest politicians.

Lynn says the engine produces 370bhp at the wheels, and there is certainly some major grunt going on. There wasn't room to let the beast fully off its leash in rural

Riverside, but Lynn was able to give it some throttle and some space to make its point a few times. It's as you would expect: a blast of action and noise, hit the back of the seats, bang into the next gear, same blast of noise and fury, same push, then bang into third and time to hit the brakes before somebody calls the cops.

Retro drag rods are often finished to a very high standard, and this one is no exception. The extensive steel fabrication on the front end has all been carried out to perfection inside and out, with the front-end panels all welded together first and then the whole assembly altered as one unit. Welding the wings, valance and bonnet together has also given a seamless line to the whole front of the car: it's a Mini, Jim, but not as we know it.

Apart from the front end, the shell remains stock 1961 Mini. It must have been tempting to stretch the pickup bed and sides to get a bit more chassis length, and to take a couple of inches off the roof when the car was being built, but the temptation was resisted and the Mini remains spiritually a Mini, although it's definitely speeding off to the madder end of the spectrum.

Tech

ENGINE – 1965 Chevrolet Corvette 327 V8, overbored 30 thou, blueprinted, with Corvette Fuellie (early fuel injection) grind cam, Edelbrock aluminium heads, Carter AFB carb with K&N filter on Weiand inlet manifold, high-output 50K coil, custom headers and cooling system. 370bhp at the wheels.

TRANSMISSION – General Motors 200RH overdrive autobox by Art Carr. Rear end, Ford 9in diff with 4.11:1 final drive ratio.

SUSPENSION – Front, single transverse spring, adjustable shocks, leading links. Rear, four-bar link with coilover shocks. Rack and pinion steering.

BRAKES – Front, 11in discs. Rear, standard Ford drums.

WHEELS AND TYRES – Front, American Racing rims, 135 x 15 Michelins. Rear, American Racing wheels, 26 x 10.5 x 15in Mickey Thompson ET street-legal cut slicks.

INTERIOR – Custom vinyl bench seating, custom steering wheel and pedals, Auto Meter gauges, Genie shifter.

EXTERIOR – Louvred and drooped one-piece flip bonnet and front end extended by 5in, tubbed rear pickup bed.

↑ The custom-trimmed cabin is mostly stuffed full of the back end of the engine and a huge automatic gearbox. Drivers with big feet need not apply. Half-cut steering wheel is inconvenient but cool. If you get far enough out of line to need much steering input on the strip, you're in the poo anyway.

↑ Traditional California rodding themes and quality standards have been applied. They'd be a cliché on a '57 Chevy but they look amazing on a Mini.

← No poncy drama-queen clouds of blue smoke and black lines on the road: just a brief roar, and the Mini is gone.

Carmelie

◥This is top-class bodywork. All the panels fit perfectly, the paint is fab and the pinstriping finishes it off just right.

Most Minis that start out being built for wives and girlfriends finish up with 1380 engines, rollcages and one seat, and are taken off the road each winter for a rebuild to go even faster. Donnie Neron's wife Carmelie LaFlamme is a lucky girl – she's actually going to get her hands on this one. Pretty soon. Honestly.

Like many of the best mad Minis it started off as scrap. This approach relieves the builder of any guilt for chopping it up, and confers a real freedom. Rather sad that California rod builders require immaculate classic cars to scrap: Mini enthusiasts are very reluctant to chop up a good Mini.

In this case, the scrap Mini's bottom half was see-through, but the roof was still solid. That's just as well, because the roof has now become the tonneau panel at the back. There's not much of the original shell left – replacement panels include the wings, nose, bonnet, A-panels, sills, floors, quarters, rear panel and valances.

A Mini is a deceptively simple-looking shape, and you find out just how subtly complex it is when you start cutting and shutting any aspect of it. Mini roof chops are inevitably more complex than they look, and although the roof looks about the same size as the back end of the car, it's not. It's a lot smaller. So when Donnie cut the roof off and tried to lay it across the rear end, it fell right through. To make it fit, he had to weld in a strip several inches wide across the middle, and butt-welding sheet metal through a long, smooth curve without warping it is a long and tricky bodywork task. He also had to follow the quite dramatic double curve of the roof panel, and deal with the significant amount of droop towards the back edge.

The old corner fuel tank has been replaced with a 15-gallon racing fuel cell in the safest place on the car, in the middle behind the bulkhead, and it's now reached by a flush-mounted filler cap. When the hole for the cap was originally drilled in the freshly-finished tonneau panel, it was about ¼in off to one side, and there was some argument about whether that mattered. 'Let's go get Carmelie, and see if she can spot it,' said Donnie. Carmelie was duly fetched and invited to inspect the back end.

'Why's the hole not in the middle?' she asked.

They can be so cruel, can't they?

Much of the rest of the custom rear bodywork was made from bits of surplus roof, but a lot of it was scratch-built from flat sheet steel literally beaten into shape with hammers and dollies on a bag of sand.

Donnie recommends a plasma cutter as a top tool, because it allows you to make tidy, accurate and smooth-edged cuts, rather than the usual chewed edge you get from trying to cut curves with shears, or the rather approximate shortened and frayed edge you get from cutting with a grinder.

⬇ Small fat bum and small fat wheels are a combo that works a treat from a styling viewpoint.

← A lot of work and time has gone into this interior, with all the colours matched and blended. Relocating the indicator switches to the gear lever has reduced interior clutter to a minimum.

↙ Frisky Cooper-inspired 1275 is also detailed to the max: it probably doesn't even leak oil.

As this was genuinely going to be Carmelie's car, it had to have doors: women prefer to retain the knicker-flashing option for special occasions, rather than doing it every time they get into their car. Standard Mini doors don't offer much in the way of side-protection or stiffness, though, particularly in the US, where the last new Mini was imported in 1967. Later Canadian Minis make some attempts at door bars and anti-intrusion arrangements, but this isn't a Canadian Mini.

With the roof becoming history but doors and therefore door apertures still in the picture, the monocoque was as floppy as a wet paper bag – so proper side bars were inevitable, and they're at a good height for protection. Donnie carried on with the safety/structural cage throughout the car, connecting the front, back and sides of the frame. The final structure of this convertible is a lot stiffer than a standard Mini monocoque, and the bodywork is attached to the internal frame to stiffen it up even more. Good structural stiffness means better suspension location and therefore better handling as well as a safe structure, as the suspension is mounted to a stable and rigid platform and operates exactly as designed.

Many mad Mini makers go for much bigger wheels, but this is ultimately a girly car, and the retention of fat little 10in wheels accentuates the Mini's fat little bum. I don't know whether Donnie figured this out consciously or subconsciously or just got lucky, but cars with fat bums make girls' bums look slimmer by comparison. I have yet

→ The rebuilding had to start before the car was completely dismantled, or it would just have been a pile of disconnected bits that would have needed a jig to assemble it.

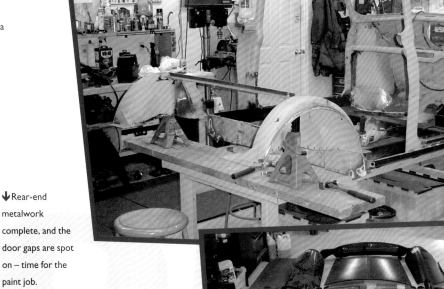

↘Here's the pile of new panels. That'll just leave the screen frame and the roof from the old body, then.

↓Rear-end metalwork complete, and the door gaps are spot on – time for the paint job.

to meet a woman who objects to something that makes her bum look slim.

The finish and paint job are seriously nice, and the choice of colours is interesting and also effective. A little delicate pinstriping adds to the effect.

As the inside of any Speedster is very much on display, it had to be special. The main focal point is the dashboard, which has a cast aluminium Dakota Digital hot-rod instrument set. This offers speedo, tacho, oil pressure, water temp, volts and fuel, as well as more esoteric electronic functions – gearshift light, maximum rpm recall, max speed recall, 0–60 time and quarter-mile time. Donny's custom GRP dash in which the Dakota gauges are mounted has two mid-range speakers pointed right at you, which are backed up by a 12in sub behind the seats. So while a couple of hundred watts of Nelly Furtado at her finest might send a shiver up your spine, the same spine will get a nice massage from the bass.

The colour of the Mountney steering wheel was chosen to complement the paint colours, and the wooden door tops and trim are stained to match. Matching the colours and tones of steering wheels and other interior woodwork is something that many people don't bother doing, and if they don't make the effort, any darker wood colours in the dash or trim have the unfortunate effect of making the wheel rim look very much like the cheap plywood from which it's actually made. A little matched staining and we're sitting in expensive furniture rather than a DIY superstore.

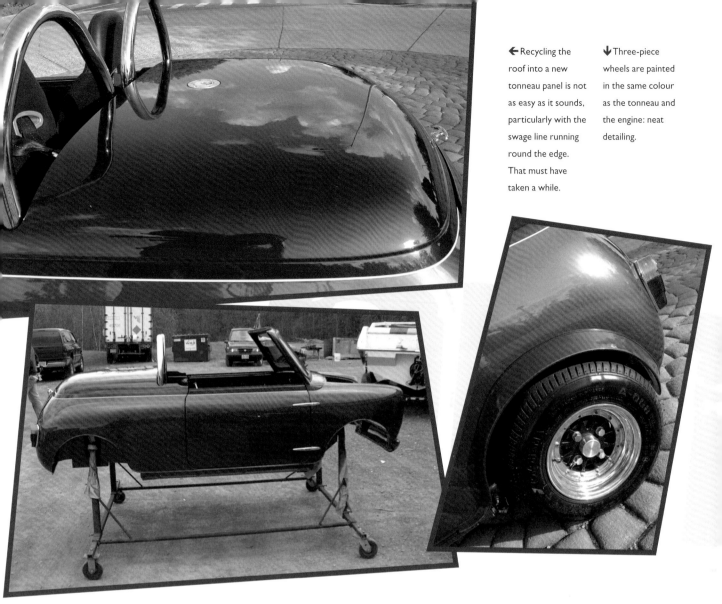

←Recycling the roof into a new tonneau panel is not as easy as it sounds, particularly with the swage line running round the edge. That must have taken a while.

↓Three-piece wheels are painted in the same colour as the tonneau and the engine: neat detailing.

↑The shell had to be painted before assembly, as the inside as well as the outside is show quality. Putting it back together without scratching the paint must have been a bit hard on the nerves...

The steering column in this car is also cool – it's been reduced to a minimalist steel tube, and the stalk functions have been relocated to the gear lever knob, which has microswitches operating the indicators, horn and fan. More electrical fun includes mirror-mounted indicator repeaters, billet number-plate holders with built-in lighting, and a third brake light. The wiring loom is custom, which is a scary idea for a lot of people. It's built around a 14-fuse panel with built-in flashers and relays, so there are no Lucas wiring parts in the car at all – the ghost of Joseph Lucas has been completely exorcised. In truth, it's only corroded and elderly British wiring that should scare anyone, as electricity running along new Lucas-spec wires in a newly built car running between new components nearly always follows the laws of physics – not always, but nearly always. Whereas the kind of grumpy old electricity that inhabits ancient Mini looms regards the laws of physics as a set of slightly impertinent suggestions, and frequently ignores them just on principle.

Donnie has remained faithful to the A-series engine, and Carmelie's powerplant is an overbored 1275 Austin America engine, which we would know in the UK as the Morris/Austin 1300. In this case it's much improved for reliability, and given enough power to provide plenty of entertainment to match the character of the car.

The state of tune is actually an excellent balance, taking the engine as far as it will go before it starts becoming temperamental and fussy. The two carbs, the big bore, the high compression ratio and the 266 cam get the most out of the engine but leave it usable in traffic with a reasonable tickover, and planting your throttle foot gets an enthusiastic response. On the other hand, the electronic ignition, forged pistons, balancing and even the electric fan will mean few worries about reliability even when the car's given the spanking it asks for. I can't think of anything I don't like about this car, apart from it being in Carmelie and Donnie's garage rather than mine.

Tech

ENGINE – Austin America block with centre main strap, 1,275cc plus 40 thou rebore. 11.5:1 compression ratio, forged pistons with 6cc dish, lightened and balanced internals. Kent 266 cam, Cooper S forged rockers, Isky dual valve springs, ported and polished Cooper S 11-stud head (12G 940) with big valves. Pertronix electronic ignition, Accel high-energy coil. Taylor 8mm silicone plug leads, side entry distributor cap, NGK BP6ES plugs. Dual 1.5in SU carbs on ported intakes, K&N air filters, LCB exhaust manifold, custom welded piping, stainless Stebro muffler, Ractive stainless oval tailpipe. Two-core rad, electric fan, polished alloy overflow tank.

TRANSMISSION – Lightened backing plate and flywheel, Rally clutch plate, Grey diaphragm pressure plate, central oil pickup, 3.44:1 final drive.

BRAKES – Single line with servo, braided lines, adjustable proportioning valve. Front, 7.5in grooved discs, Mini Spares four-pot calipers, Green Stuff pads. Rear, Cooper S drums.

SUSPENSION – Alloy box section suspension frame in rear, Spax coilovers all round, quickrack.

WHEELS AND TYRES – CMS 10in three-piece modular alloys, anodised centres, polished rims, stainless nuts, Yokohama A008 165/70 x 10.

INTERIOR – Cobra seats, Schroth three-point detachable harnesses. Nine-point custom rollcage with removable chrome hoops. Mountney wheel. Dakota Digital instrument cluster, smoothed steering column, handmade door inserts, Racerboy gear-lever-mounted indicators, horn, fan switches. Newton Commercial carpets. Alpine sound system: CDA9811, Orion four-channel amp, Earthquake SW5 12in sub, Clarion Pro Audio 5.25in mids, custom amp box, sub box, head unit mount. Remote-controlled LED lighting, microwave alarm system, custom 14-fuse wiring loom, billet aluminium illuminated licence plate frames.

EXTERIOR – Virtually all panels replaced. Chopped top, de-seamed shell. Shaved bumpers, door handles. Custom bootlid, floor, inner quarter panels, flush fuel filler, modified valance, chromed hinges. Paint, Plymouth Prowler Orange and Audi Hibiscus red, with pinstripes.

⬇ The final result is stiffer than a standard full-roofed Mini monocoque, so hurtling round a roundabout for a photo session is no bother at all.

Trikes

↓ The Mosquito/Triad was interesting as a design, and from some angles looked quite convincing.

→→ I have to admit that shooting it from directly side-on was unkind. The front end is empty, as the Mini subframe ends just in front of the wheels. Still, if you like eccentric fun and attention you couldn't do better.

Q228 FDD

I rely on producing many crap ideas amongst which is the occasional gem. One of the crap ideas was the Brookland Swallow. Actually it was a pretty good idea with one major fault. It was a 2+2 Mini-based three-wheeler, with French-British-Italian design influences: the front was inspired by Facel Vega and by Farina Rileys and Wolseleys, and the back, made from the back end of a crashed Volvo P1800, had Michelotti/Triumph Herald fins.

The Swallow's major fault was legal rather than dynamic (it actually drove very well, and the back end never misbehaved despite enthusiastic test-driving abuse) and its terminal problem became apparent at the marketing stage. The backbone of the marketing plan was to take the prototype to a kit car show and see if anybody fancied it. They did, big time, and that was when the fatal flaw was revealed – it was too heavy to be a lightweight motor tricycle and would have had to be classified as a three-wheeled car. I drive trikes for fun and because the better Morgan-inspired examples are like motorbikes that don't fall over, but many Brits drive trikes and Reliants because they don't have a full car licence. On a bike licence you can legally drive a lightweight trike under 1,000lb, but not a Mini-based affair with a cast iron engine, steel Mini doors, wind-up glass windows and a 7in x 4in perimeter steel chassis with sheet steel bulkheads and floors. Continuing the project would have meant redesigning the whole thing as a two-seater with no doors and a Citroën engine. Then the owners of the remnants of the Brooklands property

sent some greedy patent lawyer creatures after me because of the Brookland name being close to Brooklands, and that was the end of it. I haven't been back to the Brooklands museum since then, as the episode left an unpleasant taste. Cars I've designed and built since then are called Ayrspeeds. The single Swallow made it into history in Chris Rees's book on three-wheelers, but was then scrapped.

Malvern Autocraft's Triad was madder than the Swallow, and had a tiny but enthusiastic audience. It began with a competition one-off that evolved into Robert Moss's Mosquito: six were built and then the project was shelved. A Hereford motorcycle shop, Mead and

15

◣ The cabin of the Triad was a nice place to be, at least in the summer: despite the flat windscreen, the buffeting from sidewinds wasn't bad at all.

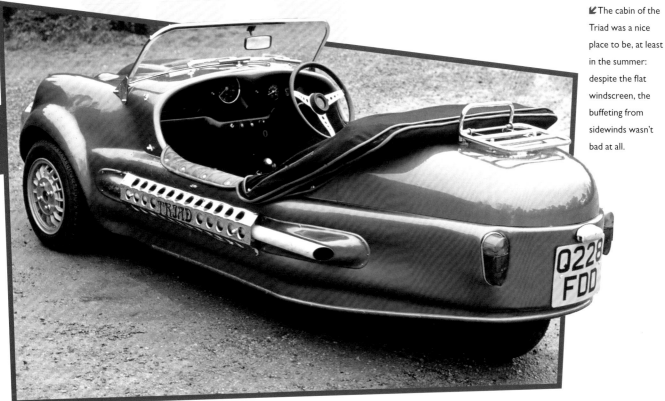

←↑ Realisation of the sketches in 3D with bits of Mini wings and doors and Volvo rear end involved compromises. But with a lighter screen frame, two-tone paint and a chrome bumper it would have looked not bad. Flip front conceals the wipers: I never liked exposed wipers.

↓ Lancia and Facel Vega meets Wolseley, but only on Planet Iain. Initial sketches for the Swallow.

↘ The rear fins were going to be quite subtle, as originally conceived. With trikes, more length means more stability, hence the long tail.

← Later sketches include the Renault 5 screen and frame, Herald-style fins and hooded headlamps.

Tomkins, took over in 1984 and built three more. Then around 1990 Rick Jones and Ian Browse formed Malvern Autocraft, updated the design a little, and relaunched the car as the Triad. The 'Warrior' competition version weighed 826lb, roughly 50% of the weight of a Mini, so driving a lightweight 1275 Triad would be like driving a 2,550cc Mini. I reviewed one for a kit car magazine, and it was a nice little car, although the styling was bizarre. But what the hell – let's have bizarre rather than dull any day.

Sandy Fraser, whom we've already met in Chapter 5, spotted the design opportunities offered by the compact and self-contained Mini engine/box/subframe/axles unit in the late 1960s, and started making three-wheelers with Mini mechanicals and largely wooden bodies in 1969. They had hardwood frames skinned in mahogany-faced marine plywood, and they drove very well.

Not many people bought them, because they were over the weight limit to drive with a motorcycle licence, but the trike, which was called the AF Spider, was slimmed down to scrape under the weight limit and a few were constructed over the next few years. The original flat wooden wings were replaced by cycle wings and the project began to take on the look of a Morgan. About a dozen were made altogether.

I've saved the best for last, though, which is The Stimson Scorcher. Barry Stimson is actually a talented car designer. He has never been in the box in the first place, and didn't need any encouragement to think outside it. He's currently designing very clever mini-motorhomes in which you can open the back window, go outside and use the cooker as a barbie. Previous to that, he was making ingenious ultra-economical little Romahome motorhomes out of Citroën saloon vans and tiny Japanese Daihatsu and Suzuki trucks. He's also now making new buggies and superbike-based trikes.

Barry is bored with hearing about the Scorcher, and wishes everybody would forget about it. Sorry, mate, no chance. The Scorcher is completely, sublimely mad. Most people would have sketched it, sniggered and gone back to work. Barry started manufacturing it instead. A few nutters bought Scorchers, and many later nutters still revere them. They have a Mini subframe and mechanicals at the front, and a single trailing wheel at the back, which is fine, but it all goes downhill from there. The Scorcher is the least practical vehicle ever made, and combines the disadvantages of both a motorcycle and a car. The driver/rider and passengers sit in the open, astride a backbone, getting wet when it rains, and then when they get where they're going the Scorcher is as big as a car so they have to pay for a parking meter.

← Plywood sheets, being somewhat flat, impose both restrictions and opportunities for styling and design.

↓ Mad but cool. If you like the idea of riding a motorbike but would prefer not to be crippled when you T-bone a Volvo, build a Mini trike and get some bugs in your teeth.

↑ A long Mini-based three-wheeler like this may look absurd, but the handling is astonishingly competent, safe and stable.

→ Barry Stimson's Stimson Scorcher, possibly the maddest Mini ever: the only answer to the obvious question as to why, is … why not?
(Courtesy of Barry Stimson)

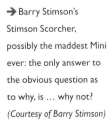

The Multicultural Mini

Akshay Crimmins is as exotic a mixture as his car: he's an Irish Indian American, and his car's a mental Japanese British Honda Clubman. His wife Jacqueline is patient and supportive although she doesn't get it, and she's an American American. The Mini was mostly built in Britain, and finished off in the California desert near Edwards Air Force Base. Now it's being written about by a Scotsman who lives in Canada, for a book published in Britain. Got a grip on all that?

OK, the story starts with Jacqueline being posted by the USAF to Norfolk, and naturally husband Akshay went along as well. When in Britain, the natural thing to do is to play with fast Minis, and that's what Akshay did. A Clubman Estate is quite rare and interesting in the USA, but in England it's traditionally been regarded as about as exciting as Wolverhampton. A rusty Clubman Estate is pretty much at the top of the list of stuff that most people don't want to buy, so Akshay didn't have to fight anybody off to get his hands on it. The bodywork was fairly horrible, with much lacework around the bottom few inches of the car, and the floors and A-panels crumbled like damp Hobnobs. The car finished up in the end looking even tastier than Hobnobs, though. The rather fab orange is Lotus Chrome Orange set off with a black roof and a walnut interior. More reminiscent of the colour scheme of a Jaffa Cake than a Hobnob, come to think of it, if we're in a bikky-metaphor mood. The orange paint works nicely with the burr walnut dash and door cappings, and the instrumentation is all Auto Meter and pretty comprehensive. Switchgear looks

remarkably aircrafty, but then Akshay used to work on USAF transport planes for a living, so that makes sense.

The early stages of the build took place in the UK, which was the best place to acquire the car, collect some cheap assorted bargain bits and pieces, and buy the necessary 15 or so Heritage panels – all at reasonable UK prices. Reasonable? Oh, yes. Mint Rover Recaro seats, 50 quid, a Schroth three-point harness for ten quid, and a second-hand Safety Devices multipoint rollcage for a hundred. Being in the UK also meant paying no import duty, shipping and US taxes on the replacement body panels, although VAT in the UK remained pretty brutal.

Also fairly cheaply available in the UK was the Metro Turbo engine, which was the first replacement engine that went in the car. Akshay is a part-time student and also a part-time test driver for Hyundai: test-driving Hyundais doesn't mean pootling along to Costcutter or Lidl the way genuine Hyundai owners will do, it means thrashing the hell out of them until they break. Akshay was actually picked for this job because he's a natural at torturing cars, and also because he's articulate enough to provide useful information as the smoking remains are hauled away. A lady vicar might be able to keep a Metro Turbo going for a while, but Akshay destroyed that engine fairly quickly, and moved on to a Honda on the basis that it would be strong enough to take a joke. The engine has been fine so far, although Akshay has managed to destroy a few springs and poked the back suspension up through the reinforced body mounts.

⬇ Akshay offers no practical reason as to why the back wheels are wider than the fronts, he just thinks it looks nice that way. On a 34bhp Mini it would look a bit Carlos Fandango, but with nitrous and a 220bhp Honda engine he can fit any wheels he likes.

16

the bigger Japanese motor. In any case, the square front only really looks weird on the round and curvy little Mini saloon shell: it looks fine on a square Estate shell.

The Clubman's inner wings were chopped out and the bulkhead was modified to make plenty of room for the Honda's quite large intake system at the back of the engine. If you're prepared to cut out the bulkhead to make room for the large standard Honda air intake it might be worth doing, as the intake is quite carefully designed and doesn't benefit from having a couple of inches rudely chopped out of it. Shortened B series manifolds still work okay, but not 100%. With the Honda motor we do have a few bhp to spare, though.

The front valance was modified quite a lot to provide better cooling, and there's an extra oil cooler used for water cooling, because by this time Uncle Sam had tapped Jacqueline on the shoulder in the UK and had told her that California was her next home. Edwards Air Force Base is in the Mojave Desert, which gets seriously baked in the summer. It's also seriously empty quite a lot of the time, and there's one small road that just disappears into the desert, which is where we took the car out to play. The road apparently goes in a straight line for a few hundred miles and finishes up in Las Vegas, but nobody was using it.

OK, Akshay, how fast does your Clubman go? First it shreds a bit of tyre tread, then gets a grip and screams up to 5,000rpm, at which point there's a bang, a jerk and the dual cams slap in another big chunk of power up to about 9,000. Several driveshafts have been snapped or corkscrewed in the search for a pair that would survive an Akshay take-off, and the current pair from Watson Rally are surviving well. He slaps it into second and floors it again. More blattering noise, more gear whine, the cams bang in again and torque-steer visibly twitches the steering wheel. Third gear, fourth and fifth, and the entire structure is vibrating and banging as the desert landscape hurtles past in a blur. Can't focus on the speedometer at this speed, because the road's too bumpy: the needle's gone right round and more, though. OK, this is quite fast. Unlike the SR-71 Blackbird, the Clubman is neither stealthy nor radar-invisible, so it's surprising Akshay still has a licence.

In standard form, the B-series 1.8-litre Vtec engine as fitted to Honda saloons such as the Integra puts out between 140 and 215bhp, so in a light Mini shell the engine provides more fun than when Coyote caught the Roadrunner ("Fxxxxxx beep beep now, ya xxxxx"). The variable cam geometry allows for civilised and economical pootling about at low revs, but if you leave your foot on it and let the revs get going, the camshaft profiles change quite violently as the cam lobes change from mild to wild, and maximum power suddenly piles in. The Vtec system works by providing two cam lobes for each valve: at low

↑ The Honda engine looks quite at home. Plenty of room for a turbocharger in there as well. 34,000lb of thrust is quite frisky – oh, hang on, that's the SR-71, not the Honda.

The suspension is by coilovers with Gaz shocks. Tough enough for most people driving a Mini saloon, but with Akshay's driving and the additional weight of the Clubman's Estate back end with its rear doors and all the extra glass, one of the springs couldn't take it and let go. Its replacement has been fine so far.

For a car this quick, decent brakes are a necessity, and fortunately Metro Turbo four-pots with EBC Green Stuff pads and grooved and cross-drilled discs are well up to the task and didn't break the bank. They don't have shiny ally calipers and cool brand badges, but they do slow the car down from jail speeds very quickly, with no bother at all.

There was talk of converting the square front end to round Mini front end panels on styling grounds, but it didn't make much sense to replace the front end with a whole bunch of new panels and then chop it all up to extend it for the Honda engine, when the car was a Clubman already with plenty of room at the front for speeds, the smaller-profile, rounder cam lobes open the valves a small amount for a short time, providing low power, a smooth tickover and good economy. As the revs rise, a pin driven by rising oil pressure locks in a second cam lobe with a much sharper and higher profile. This holds the valves open wider and for longer, throwing lots more air and fuel through the engine – which is the key to more performance.

The added bang of power provides torque-steer violent enough to rip the steering wheel out of your hands if you're not firmly hanging on to it, and people are now developing ECU software changes to soften the cam change for Mini Vtec conversions.

Naturally this engine at around 170bhp wasn't fast enough or violent enough for Akshay, so he rebuilt

his Honda motor with a 20-thou overbore and higher compression Type-R USDM (United States Dealer Market) Honda pistons, changed the cams for a pair of Stage 1 Skunk2 items, ported and polished the head and inlet manifold, gas-flowed the valve seats with three angles and changed the ECU for a Skunk2 that lets the engine get much closer to its real power limits. Even if you don't buy all your performance goodies from the same good-quality tuning company, which is the best option for uprating

↓ It's too risky to let me on an airliner with a nail-clipper, but taking pictures on an active USAF base is no problem. Go figure.

↑ Rear plate bears American, Indian, British and Japanese flags. Akshay is an Irish Indian American, which probably makes him a tribe of one.

↓ If you see a nitrous oxide bottle this size, it means the owner actually uses it. Be afraid, be very afraid.

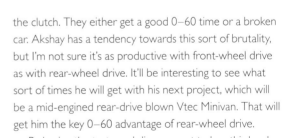

↑ The serious rollcage visible in this Mini not only keeps you in one piece if the poo hits the fan, but stiffens the whole shell and sharpens up the handling significantly.

engines, it's a good idea to match components where you can – so getting the cams from Skunk2 and matching them with a Skunk2 ECU was well worthwhile. You already know that they've been developed to work together without any conceptual or engineering mismatches.

With nitrous oxide you need a big fat clean spark, so ignition is now MSD 6-AL with 9mm plug leads and cold platinum plugs. The cat has strayed, as there's no need for a catalytic converter on a 1975-registered car in California, which has ferocious environmental laws on newer cars but so far leaves old ones alone to a great extent. We just have to hope the current scare story switches back from global warming to global cooling and the next New Ice Age before all amusing cars are banned. In ten years our political types will be squealing fashionably for all the carbon dioxide they can get to feed the rainforest and stop the glaciers from covering Alaska.

Akshay's exhaust is an appalling ecological disaster – a simple four-into-two-into-one with a single fat silencer at the end. His final power figure is about 220bhp, as his mods are all designed to be productive rather than cosmetic, and his nitrous set-up is a 50-shot kit with a big bottle adding another 50 usable horsepower, so we're looking at something like 270bhp at full chat. No wonder the Clubman is a bit nippy.

His plan for the next stage with the engine is a turbocharger… so the car's current 4.5 seconds to 60mph time is going to look pretty lazy after the turbo goes in. The exhaust manifold is at the front of the engine, so there are plenty of options for turbo placement. He's serious about this: with a decent-sized turbo it will add another 150bhp to make 400bhp+.

0–60mph times in production cars tend to be achieved by test drivers selecting first gear, bouncing the engine revs off the rev limiter and then sliding their foot sideways off

the clutch. They either get a good 0–60 time or a broken car. Akshay has a tendency towards this sort of brutality, but I'm not sure it's as productive with front-wheel drive as with rear-wheel drive. It'll be interesting to see what sort of times he will get with his next project, which will be a mid-engined rear-drive blown Vtec Minivan. That will get him the key 0–60 advantage of rear-wheel drive.

By having the taste and discernment to buy this book, you've made a valuable contribution to the chance of *More Mad Minis* being published, and if that happens Akshay's next build will be high on the list of contents. Watch this space, as they say.

Tech

ENGINE – 20-thou overbored 1,834cc Honda Vtec DOHC B18 block with balanced, micro-polished crank, USDM Type-R high-comp pistons (10.9:1), new stock rods, Stage 1 Skunk2 cams with AEM adjustable timing gears. Ported, polished head with three-angled valve seats, ported inlet manifold, 4-2-1 exhaust manifold, de-catted exhaust with single tail box. AEM fuel rail and pressure regulator. Skunk2 OBD-I ECU with OBD-II harness by LocashRacing.com, MSD 6-AL ignition with external coil. 9mm plug leads, cold platinum plugs. ZEX 50-shot nitrous oxide kit. Oil cooler. Standard Honda radiator with slim FAL electric fan, additional oil cooler used as booster rad for coolant. External MSD fuel pump.

TRANSMISSION – Lightened aluminium flywheel, Stage 1 race clutch. Honda LS Integra gearbox with high fifth gear. Watson Rally driveshafts.

BRAKES – Metro Turbo four-pot calipers with EBC Green Stuff pads, aluminium Minifins rear with EBC Green Stuff linings. Braided lines, modified brake pedal.

SUSPENSION – Gaz adjustable coilovers with custom springs, custom K-series Metro steering rack.

WHEELS AND TYRES – Custom three-piece 9lb 13in magnesium alloys by Keiser Racing, with 175/50 x 13 Dunlops.

INTERIOR – Recaro seats ex-Rover, Safety Devices rollcage, Schroth full harness, Moto-Lita steering wheel, Auto Meter 5in electronic programmable speedo, 5in monster tacho with shift light, water temp, oil pressure, oil temp, volts, fuel. Modified Honda gear lever. Burr walnut door cappings. Clarion CD, Rockford Fosgate amp, two Sony 6 x 9 speakers.

EXTERIOR – 1975 Clubman shell restored with 15 replacement Heritage panels. Front bulkhead modified, inner wings deleted. Front valance modified but retained.

↓This straight and empty road goes all the way to Las Vegas, and makes a top test track for mad Minis. Brown racing underpants are recommended.

Varnishing Point

ichael and Lorraine Mihalik are not mad as such, but they don't think the same way as most of their people-carrier-driving Seattle neighbours.

When I first saw a low-resolution picture of the Mini Woody that Michael had built to present to Lorraine, I wondered why on earth they'd painted the back panels brown. It only sank in later that the panels were actually veneered in African Mahogany.

Surely you can't veneer metal, though, can you? 'Why not?' is the answer. Most people have simply never thought of doing it. Veneering usually means sticking a thin layer of an expensive wood over a piece of cheaper wood, and then varnishing it between ten and twenty times. But if you want to stick veneer to bits of metal instead of bits of wood, there's absolutely nothing stopping you but convention.

Why would anybody want to veneer metal? Well, after you've checked out these pics you might well decide that it actually looks fab, which is a fine reason to do it. Michael's initial reason was rather more pragmatic than that, though. He spent a long time on the bodywork of this Mini, getting it straight and sorted and finally doing all the expensive and time-consuming paint prep himself to save the five grand or so it costs to get a good professional painter to sort the body surface ready for a show quality finish. Then he sent it off to the painter, who sprayed on a lovely job of Spinnaker White. Michael and Lorraine inspected it, admired it and approved it: the finished paint was superb. The next day, as

instructed, the painter went to work again and laid on another beautifully smooth coat of white on the inside of the car. Sadly, it wasn't quite the same shade of Spinnaker White as the previous day's paint on the outside of the car. Maybe it was Mainsail White, or Fore Topgallant Sail White. Pretty though the colour might have been, Spinnaker White it wasn't.

'You're going to have to do it again,' said Michael.

The painter was not entirely over the moon about that idea, as he would have had to duplicate much of Michael's months of patient prep. In the end, he suggested that Michael just take the car away and forget about paying for it. Michael did that, but was still left with a very slightly two-tone car.

That's when the veneering idea presented itself. If the interior were to be completely covered in fine wood veneers and then retrimmed in leather, it would look fabulous, although it would look like no other Mini. Which would in itself be no bad thing.

So that's the way it went. Much of the inside of a Mini

↑ A closer look reveals that what looked like brown paint is actually genuine African red mahogany veneer. It takes many varnish coats and much rubbing down to achieve this sort of depth.

17

← The side view looks strange – why are the side panels painted brown?

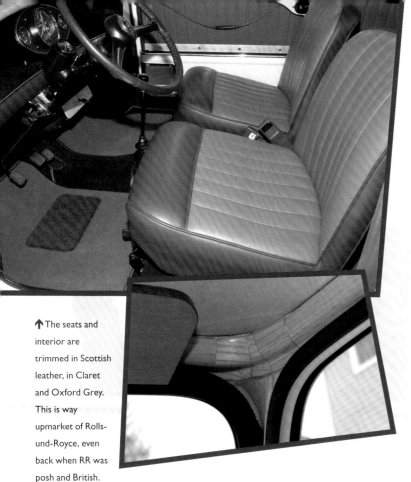

↑ The seats and interior are trimmed in Scottish leather, in Claret and Oxford Grey. This is way upmarket of Rolls-und-Royce, even back when RR was posh and British.

↗ Veneer comes in flat sheets, so covering a complex curve is what you might call challenging.

is composed of usefully flat or single curve surfaces, but where the surfaces are concavely curved, the technique is to cut triangular slices out of the veneer until the surface is covered.

For convex curves, you have to add little pizza slices and try to match the grain. The grain won't ever match up exactly when you've done that, but even so it still looks nice.

There are also quite a lot of new solid pieces of wood inside the car, specifically custom-carved for it – the heater panel and the sun-visors are solid ash wood, as are the strips across the roof and in the loading bay. Mind you, nobody is going to be throwing toolboxes into the back, so the ash floor strakes are mostly decorative.

The couple's expertise in woodwork comes from owning and restoring an ancient 1948 MG over a couple of decades. The MG is of the coachbuilt type that was made from a separate steel chassis and a thin metal skin over an ash frame. The couple also run a Land Rover, so they're well versed in the vicissitudes of classic British rust. With the MG, they not only had to deal with the familiar scenario of crumbling steel, but also with woodworm, assorted hungry boring insects enjoying a tasty and nicely-matured wood banquet, dry rot and wet rot – so after dealing successfully with that, a spot of planing and routing action in clean new ash was a walk in the park.

The skill and experience gained with the MG was applied to the outside woodwork on the Woody. A half-timbered Mini Traveller isn't actually a proper Woody like a Morris Minor Traveller or a Rolls-Royce shooting brake, in which the woodwork is the main structure of the back end. I suppose the Rolls shooting brakes and their descendants must be the origin of the term Estate Car in the first place, as they were actually used on estates. A Mini Woody is actually a steel estate car body, a Minivan variant with some decorative woodwork glued on top. This is good rather than bad news, as the whole structure is less prone to rotting and collapsing. I once had a Morris Minor Traveller with a delightful little glade of mushrooms and mosses growing in the damp and rotting wooden rear window tracks, but I wouldn't have dared open any of the windows, as they were all that was holding the roof up. As the Morris was crumbling audibly with its last MOT on the horizon and was not long for this world anyway, I used to water the little garden if it began to look dry.

Something to remember if you're ever rebuilding a Mini Woody is to allow any new ash parts you've bought to dry out and season for at least a year, and preferably two, because if you varnish the wood with any dampness still inside, it's like sealing fruit into a plastic bag: it will rot from the inside out.

With the exterior woodwork seasoned, sorted out and coated in 13 layers of marine urethane varnish, the next step was to get the interior carpentry and decor up to a matching standard. The result was a retrim in grey and burgundy leather, which looks and smells seriously nice. It has something of a 1960s Wood & Pickett feel to it, but the interior veneering and custom woodwork puts it into a different league. The grey suede custom headlining looks pretty sweet too.

The car was built for local and highway use as well as for show. One reason for the necessary highway capability is that Michael and Lorraine have to drive on Interstate 5 as it passes through Seattle. Speeds on the section of Interstate Highway 5 that stampedes through the Seattle conurbation average a bumper-to-bumper 85mph with seven lanes charging each way – it's illegal by 30mph over the limit, but who's going to stop them? There are some substantial hills, and many dumb and impatient rednecks tailgating you in vast shiny chest-wig pickups. The Mini therefore needed a serious engine, but Michael and Lorraine fancied spending a little time without black fingernails so they bought a built engine from Mini Mania, with a Longman head, an Elgin cam and Powermax pistons, an Aldon Yellow distributor and enough cooling to deal with summer trips to the desert in the southern parts of California. The electric cooling fan is automatic, but has a manual override switch in case of nervousness. Flywheel bhp is 113 with 102lb/ft of torque, which is enough to provide relaxed agility and to keep up with even Seattle's mad highway speeds.

The drum brakes also had to be upgraded, but they wanted to stick with the correct steel 10in wheels, so the only option was a set of Cooper discs. Not cheap, but they do the business and still fit inside the little wheels, so job done.

All was sorted, fine and dandy, but then Michael, newly freed from the bounds of convention, had another off-the-wall idea. He wanted to make a roof-rack out of bits of chromed kitchen plumbing tube, which would involve drilling 26 holes in the freshly painted roof to fit it. He approached Lorraine with this scheme.

'I got this idea. I want to add a roof rack, like the old '40s woodies.'

'No way, you're not doing that on my car. You're NOT doing that on my car. I'm having nothing to do with it. Idiot.'

Gentle pressure prevailed, and although drilling 26 holes in the gleaming new paint provided a few nervous moments, you can see how well it worked out. The rack is ingeniously made from copper kitchen piping and fittings. By making split wooden templates and then gradually bolting the two halves together with the piping inside, the copper was gently curved to the right shape. Heat-sink mud was used to stop heat transfer, so that the rest of the roof rack didn't come unsoldered and fall apart as each new joint was soldered. Chrome plating involves a copper coating anyway, so solid copper pipe as it comes is already perfectly prepped to go into the chroming tanks. Solder can also be chromed: the chrome plating process is cold, so the soldered joints were unaffected and the rack came out completely intact, to provide the perfect finishing touch on an impressive Mini project.

Tech

ENGINE – 1,380cc by Mini Mania, 73.5mm Powermax pistons, Elgin cam, Longman GT6 head. Aldon Yellow distributor, HIF6 SU carb with BDK needle, Maniflow LCB, double core radiator, auxiliary electric fan. 113 crank bhp @ 6,500rpm, 102lb/ft @ 4,700rpm.

TRANSMISSION – Standard four-speed, 3.11:1 final drive ratio. Rod change gear lever extension.

BRAKES – Braided lines, plastic Lockheed master cylinder reservoir. Front, Cooper S discs and calipers, Mintex pads. Rear, standard.

SUSPENSION – Standard.

WHEELS AND TYRES – Standard 10in steels, 145 SR 10 radials.

INTERIOR – Most surfaces veneered in English white ash or African red mahogany. Seats reupholstered in Oxford Grey and Claret Scottish leather. Tacho, retractable seat belts added.

EXTERIOR – Rear lower body panels veneered in red mahogany. Custom roof rack in chromed copper tubing with English white ash slats. Thirteen coats wood varnish. Paint, base coat Spinnaker White with clearcoat over.

↑Ashtray is let into the veneered steel dash panel. The Woody is a no-smoking zone, as you might expect.

←Wooden sun visors were made from scratch. The convex mirror is rather unkind: it would make even Helena Bonham-Carter look like Winston Churchill.

↑Veneering the rear oddments box and ashtray panel is one thing, but we all know that the B-post with its awkward bulge is steel – which must have been seriously tricky to do.

The Roofless Cooper

⬎ The GRP flip front saves considerable weight and makes engine and suspension access a joy. Double front bumper is detachable and separate from the rest of the front end.

It's Jeremy's party and he can cry if he wants to. Many people would say he was completely mad to chop up an original Cooper S. He would agree with them now, but he says he was young and foolish when this project started.

'At the time I didn't have an ordinary Mini to modify so I chopped the S. Looking back I never would normally have done that, but I was young and had a hacksaw in one of my hands, so off with the top!'

There's also the point that the Cooper S as a model is much more common in the USA as a percentage of Minis than it is in the UK. That may seem odd, but the reason is that nearly all British Minis until the final decade or so were just day-to-day working 998s or whatever, which were bought as cheap transport. In the US, people who bought Minis normally bought them for fun, or for a second weekend car, or just because they were cute – so the Americans were much more likely to buy a Cooper version or a Woody. A Woody is, after all, a half-timbered car, like Shakespeare's house, so their Tudorbethan styling appealed to anglophile Americans, and still does. In the 1960s, American V8s were fast in a straight line, but a Cooper S would run rings round most of them if there were any corners involved. Of the remaining American Minis, many

are Coopers, Woodies, Wolseleys, pickups and so on.

However, any functioning Mini is a relatively rare beast in the US. It's still relatively easy in the UK – although increasingly less so – to pop out and buy an MOT-failed 998 scrapper for a few hundred quid, snatch it from the jaws of the crusher and use it as the basis for a Mad Mini, but that option simply doesn't exist in America. Even pretty horrible basket cases are rescued, as described elsewhere in this book.

In any case, before we start sticking pins in Jeremy-shaped voodoo dollies for chopping up a Cooper S, Jeremy has already been punished by the Mini Spirits. When he was loading his freshly finished Speedster on to its trailer to go to Mini Meet West in 2001, one of the extra wide flares caught on the edge of the trailer and got half torn off. The car is normally used on the road and isn't a trailer queen, but it does have a suede pigskin dashboard and no roof, so it usually goes to shows on a trailer.

Jeremy stayed up all night, repaired the wing and charged off to the show as dawn broke, thinking that karma was restored, and that he'd paid the price for chopping the S. Things certainly looked that way at the show – he won People's Choice, Car of the Show, and the autocross.

Evil spirits waited until he was doing quite well in the rally, lulled him into a false sense of security and then went for him big time. A control arm bolt fell off, and he crashed into a ditch. That sounds bad, but it was with some relief that Jeremy checked the car out and found minimal damage, even to the precious bodywork. Ace Mini mechanic Martin Webber (www.westcoastclassics.com) from the Vancouver

↑ Weber-fed 1380 packs a considerable punch, even more so as the car is missing its heavy glasshouse and roof.

↑ The poor old instruments had nowhere to go, as the Weber and its filter pushed them right back inside the car. Top gurgle-and-suck soundtrack accompanies stonking performance.

→ Second-generation Fortech wheel arches are attached with just-visible rivet heads: this is a deliberate styling choice. Revolution four-spokes in powder-coat white with machined edges are still top lookers as far as wheels go.

Mini Club is the type of bloke who always has a spare control arm bolt in his pocket, so the car was recovered from the ditch and sorted out without too much drama. The front was detached and carefully laid on a grass bank as the car was gingerly winched back up on to the road. Jeremy risked a smile of relief, and the evil spirits spotted him smiling and reactivated his punishment. The wind gusted, flipped the front upside down and dragged it right across the road on its shiny side. He won the Hard Luck award that year as well, but the spirits reckoned that enough karma payback was enough, and he was allowed to proceed with his life. The universe was back in balance again.

If any Mini fanatics are still seething and spitting over the disgraceful scalping of a rare classic, you've probably shredded this book and jumped up and down on its corpse by now, but you do have the option of buying Jeremy's car, importing it and restoring it to its original standard trim, as it's for sale.

Jeremy has owned 43 Minis, which has to make him one of the most enthusiastic American Mini enthusiasts ever. That's probably one reason why his creations get wilder and wilder as the years pass. How many Coopers can you restore without it turning into just work?

Minis offer such a contrast to big American and boring Japanese cars that, once hooked, Americans often become fanatical enthusiasts — somebody once bought a Mini from Jeremy even though a wheel fell off during the test drive. That's a pretty keen buyer.

Removing the roof of a monocoque Mini makes the

whole structure floppy as it does any other chassisless monocoque, and the further removal of the front outer and inner wings to be replaced by a GRP flip front also reduced this car's rigidity to that of a wet teddy bear.

You can put some stiffness back into an open Mini by bracing the floors and fabricating deep sills, but you really need some quite substantial steelwork to get anywhere near the structural rigidity provided by the original steel roof.

Jeremy constructed a massive frame that connects the front and back of the cabin and then extends through the bulkhead to bolt to the front of the subframe, so the car finished up much stronger than a standard shell.

The rollover bar is also part of this structure, and it's genuine rather than decorative — the main hoop is triangulated backwards to the frame, and is also braced sideways so that it can't 'lozenge' or collapse sideways. Single roll hoops behind your head are better than nothing, and useful if you just roll over, but more ambitious and enthusiastic crashing requires a rollover bar braced in at least one additional direction. The car has been reworked for 13in wheels — easy enough at the front but trickier at the back, which has been fully tubbed to suit the bigger wheels.

The car's suspension is as stiff as the rollover bar, with S Racer Red springs and Spax shocks all round. If the original unsympathetic Mini seats were still fitted, Jeremy's inaugural drive in the car would probably have terminated in the car park of his chiropractor's office, but his Corbeaux (The plural of Corbcau would have to be Corbeaux, wouldn't it?) make the ride just stiff rather than brutal. These are rare period low-back Corbeaux, hard to find in the UK never mind in the US, and they are much treasured by Jeremy.

Advice from David Vizard was adhered to when it came to porting the head on the 1380 to suit Rimflow valves, and to reworking the combustion chambers. Vizard remains one of the top Mini tuning gurus, and now lives in the US and pops up at Mini Meets sometimes: he also remains approachable and entertaining.

The big Weber carb and air filter on its huge intake came through the bulkhead and occupied all the space previously inhabited by the speedo, but Jeremy just moved the whole dash plate backwards and covered it in suede, without even boxing it in. It might look wrong in a more conventional Mini, but on this one the idea works a treat.

Braking performance is more ambitious than it is in most Minis. The system remains on an optimistic single circuit, as in the original Cooper, but the front calipers are big four-pot JFZ/SRP numbers. (JFZ were an old and respected American name in performance brakes, like Wilwood, but they were bought out by SRP.) The discs themselves are large vented Brembos. With the original 10in Cooper wheels the choice of brakes is limited and expensive, but Jeremy took advantage of the clearance offered by his 13in wheels to avail himself of the full range of brake options, and put seriously big brakes on. The car is used for autocross in coned car parks, and with big grunt and big brakes it's almost as fast as a Moke.

The soundtrack of this car is even more hardcore than the springs: it churns over slowly and then barks as it fires up, with lots of sucking and gurgling noises from the enormous Weber. You can actually hear air and fuel being sucked down the seven-inch-long intake trumpets, and the engine shakes and stumbles on idle, partly because of the cam and partly because of the inevitably rich mixture.

The high-ratio quick-rack steering combined with fat sticky Pirellis means that steering is seriously hard work at anything less than 20mph, and the engine is sulky and has to be kept going with careful use of the throttle – but all that's forgotten as the engine clears its throat and lets loose on the highway, providing joyous grunt and howl. In 100° Oregon summer heat the lack of a roof is murderous when stationary, but bliss at speed.

The security system on this car is provided by the detachable steering wheel, which you simply take with you when you go shopping. This does look daft, and there's not much chance of the car being successfully stolen anyway: it takes artistry with the throttle and clutch to get it moving, skills way beyond the driving talents of most modern crims.

Jeremy's penchant for small evil things with fat wheels extends to his Go-Ped fetish, which in a way makes sense. Oregonians can legally drive unlicensed kiddy-style scooters with little petrol engines on them, so Jeremy enthusiastically abuses this privilege by fitting these tiny things with massively powerful motors and tearing around burning rubber and popping wheelies on them. Almost as much fun as a Mini.

ENGINE – 1,380cc, lightened and balanced rods, Omega pistons and rings, Kent 530 cam. Head by Tony Lewis of Eugene, to David Vizard specs: ported, polished, Rimflow valves. Cooper S no-vacuum distributor, Pertronix ignition, NGK plugs, BumbleBee leads. 45DCOE Weber carb on 7in alloy intake, LCB exhaust manifold and single box RC40 exhaust. S pulley on stock water pump and rad. Large remote oil filter, cooler, aeroquip lines. Maybe 130–140bhp at the crank.

TRANSMISSION – Orange diaphragm with standard clutch, four-synchro close-ratio Cooper S box. 3.44:1 final drive ratio.

BRAKES – Standard single circuit, braided lines. Front, JFZ/SRP four-piston calipers on vented Brembo discs. Rear, Super Minifin drums.

SUSPENSION – S Racer adjustable Hi-Los with Red coil springs, Spax shocks. Quick rack.

WHEELS AND TYRES – 7J x 13 Revolution four-spokes, powder-coated white with polished lip, 175/50 x 13 Pirelli tyres.

INTERIOR – Rare lowback Corbeau GTA seats, 3in lap belts, quick-release Momo suede wheel, Auto Meter Pro-Comp Ultra Lite gauges in pigskin suede extended pod. KAD short shift on Cooper S remote. Newton Commercial trim and carpets.

EXTERIOR – One-piece GRP front end, Fortech Gen II wheel arches, tubbed rear end, roof removed, rollover bar and body brace structure fitted. PPG Pure Toner Orange paint.

The MADMEN

↓ Madman Allen Frost's pickup just looks like a nice Mini…

The Mid-America Diehard Mini Enthusiasts' Network enjoys that very rare thing, an acronym that works perfectly. The club is based in Missouri, inasmuch as it's based anywhere, and Missouri is absolutely mid-America.

Diehard they are too: one of the Madmen's regular trips is to drive, in mostly 40-year-old Minis, from the annual Mini Meet West gathering, usually on the Pacific coast, right across the USA to the other annual event, Mini Meet East, which is always held a few days later. In 2008 this meant driving from Los Angeles, California, to Bethel, Maine, which took the Madmen over 3,000 miles in about four days across some serious mountains in cars with solid rubber suspension. That trip would be hard work in three tons of luxury motorhome, so doing it in a Mini certainly qualifies as diehard. Mini enthusiasts? We can't argue with that description either – these people are Mini enthusiasts in the same way that Attila the Hun was a fighting enthusiast. Finally the word network accurately describes the structure or lack of structure of the organisation. The members are scattered all over the USA and Canada, and for that matter the whole world, so they can't pop down to Bubba's Greasyburgers for a club meeting on the third Tuesday of the month.

The organisation was started by Karl Strauch in 1988, when he and his three Minis moved from New England to Missouri, all piled in one moving truck along with his furniture. Three more Minis soon turned up locally, which was enough to form a club. Karl published newsletters which finished up going all over the place, and the informal club developed into a structure that Karl compares to Alcoholics Anonymous, except that the idea is to encourage new people to develop an addiction to charging around in Minis, rather than curing them of it. Like all Mini clubs, they organise treasure hunts, but there could be a thousand miles between clues.

The big idea for 2009 was a trip to Alaska, where the mosquitoes are bigger than Minis, followed straight afterwards by attendance at the 2009 East Meets West Mini Meet in Minnesota to celebrate the Mini's 50th birthday. Just going a couple of thousand miles to Minnesota and back would have been too easy.

You can't just apply to join the Madmen, though – you need to complete a continuous 5,000-mile cross-continental single trip in a Mini powered by an A-series engine, backed up by pictures and receipts. For people living in the UK, driving east for 2,500 miles would get you deep into Russia or Kazakhstan. How many Brits would casually leap into their Minis and head for Moscow?

Mini guru and author David Vizard is the honorary patron of the club, and well qualified to be a Madman, having driven a Mini on a circuit of America getting 55mpg at 55mph. A top man, he has strong and amusing opinions on pretty well everything you care to mention.

This Madness may actually be infectious: for 2008

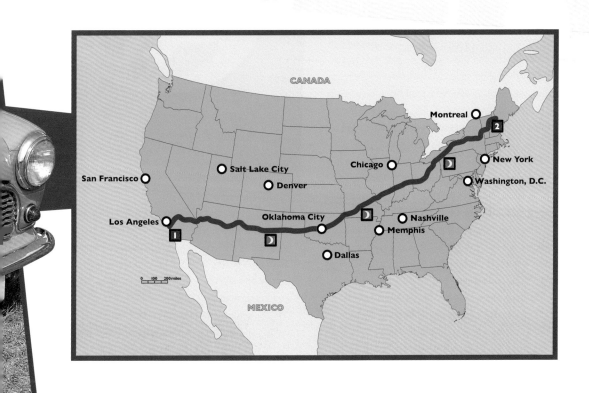

← The Madmen's route across country from Mini Meet West in Los Angeles to Bethel in Maine covers slightly over 3,000 miles in just a few days. Pedal to the metal and an oil change at either end.

...until you notice that it tows a custom-built mini-trailer with a proper gooseneck mounting in the pickup bed. It's really for rescuing the occasional dead Mini rather than a serious load carrier.

→ When the bike bounced off the side of the pickup it took out the tyre but missed the rare and expensive rim, which was a bit of luck.

I planned a trip in the Marcos Heritage Mini Marcos which would have taken me up and down the UK for a week or two touring sofas and visiting chums, then to Belgium to shoot Mad Frank's V8 big-block Mini (Chapter 21), then southwards to check out a spot of vintage racing at the Circuit des Remparts in Angoulême, then to Barcelona to check out some top mad Gaudi architecture, then along the French Riviera to Italy, then via Florence and Rome to Bari on the Adriatic coast to catch a ferry to Dubrovnik in Croatia and thence to visit the in-laws in Split, then north through Slovenia and Austria to Switzerland and Germany. Travel in Germany would have been kept brief: their roads are either hurtling tailgating nightmares or stationary car parks as tailgating's inevitable results are cleared and all the squashed slow-learners are airlifted to hospital.

Then back across blissfully empty middle France on a bit of an eating and wine-tasting tour back towards the UK (Macon burgundy tastes particularly good in Macon; I suspect they keep some of the good stuff back for the locals) to return the Marcos demonstrator and catch a plane home. Which some might say makes me as mad as the Madmen. I wouldn't disagree. In the end circumstances conspired to torpedo that plan and all I managed was the sofa tour, the Twini Mini in Birmingham, the Goodwood Revival and Mad Frank in Zeebrugge. Maybe I'll do the full tour next year: the Mini Marcos went very well.

Long-distance Mini action is not without its dramas. During the 2007 Mini Meet East near Knoxville, Tennessee, many people went for a play on a road called the Dragon's Tail. It's very wriggly, rather like your average

Welsh or Scottish Highland mountain road but with a better surface and less sheep poo. There are 318 curves in 11 miles. Americans regard corners as a fascinating novelty, and have a go at the Dragon's tail in huge numbers, frequently on big bikes that they can't handle. They fall off this road quite a lot.

Mini drivers are usually fast and competent, and of course they have the huge advantage of driving the best car in the world for whizzing round tight corners. They didn't have any problems at all on the Dragon's tail until an American biker whose confidence exceeded his competence went round a corner too fast and fell off his

bike, which then hit Madman Allen Frost's pickup-and-trailer rig. The bike bounced off the back of the Mini and then went under the trailer, while the rider went flying over the trailer. His head was still attached to his body when he stopped sliding down the road, but only because he was very, very lucky. Incredibly, the Americans still allow articulated 18-wheeler trucks on this road: I suppose it's good business for the local private ambulance service and the coroner.

The Targa Newfoundland (www.targanewfoundland.com) is a marathon rallying event that attracts assorted Madmen and usually features several Minis. Even going along as part of a support crew is demanding, as Madman Rick Higgs and his wife Elaine discovered. The event covers 1,394 miles: 1,056 are transits between stages, but 310 of those miles are full-speed competition with normal legal speed limits suspended and the roads cleared of traffic. For Vancouver entrants, that all happens only after you've driven 4,500 miles from Vancouver just to get to the event. When you get there, Newfoundland doesn't even welcome you with nice weather: it's like Scotland's Atlantic coast, very pretty when you can spot a glimpse of it through the usual sheets of driving rain.

Mad? I should say so.

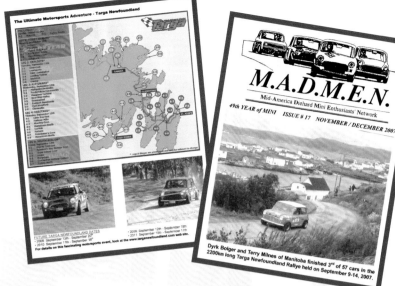

↑ The Targa Newfoundland is becoming increasingly popular. Local roads are closed and used for stages: half the fun is that you can legally drive down village main streets at 100mph during the stages that go through inhabited areas. Many competitors use relatively cheap cars, on the basis that they may not survive the rally.

Dyrk Bolger and Terry Milnes of Manitoba finished 3rd of 57 cars in the 2200km long Targa Newfoundland Rallye held on September 9-14, 2007.

↑ The Madmen's newsletter has been produced for decades: founder member Karl is taking a rest from it, so new blood will be needed.

→ The body was slightly bashed, so it was decorated with a very apt dragon design at Mini Meet East by future Mini enthusiast Emily Caldwell.

↓ Once you've proved yourself with receipts and pics, you're entitled to display the coveted badge on your Mini.

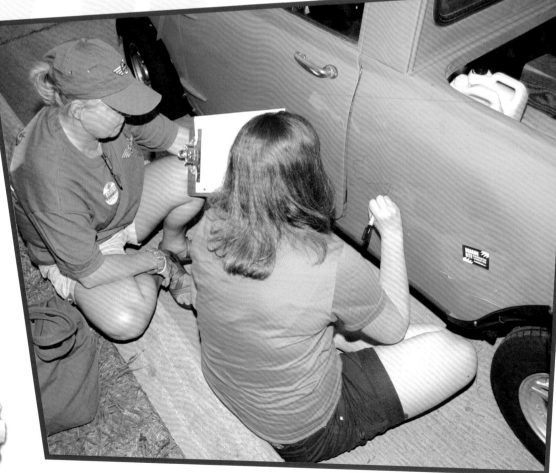

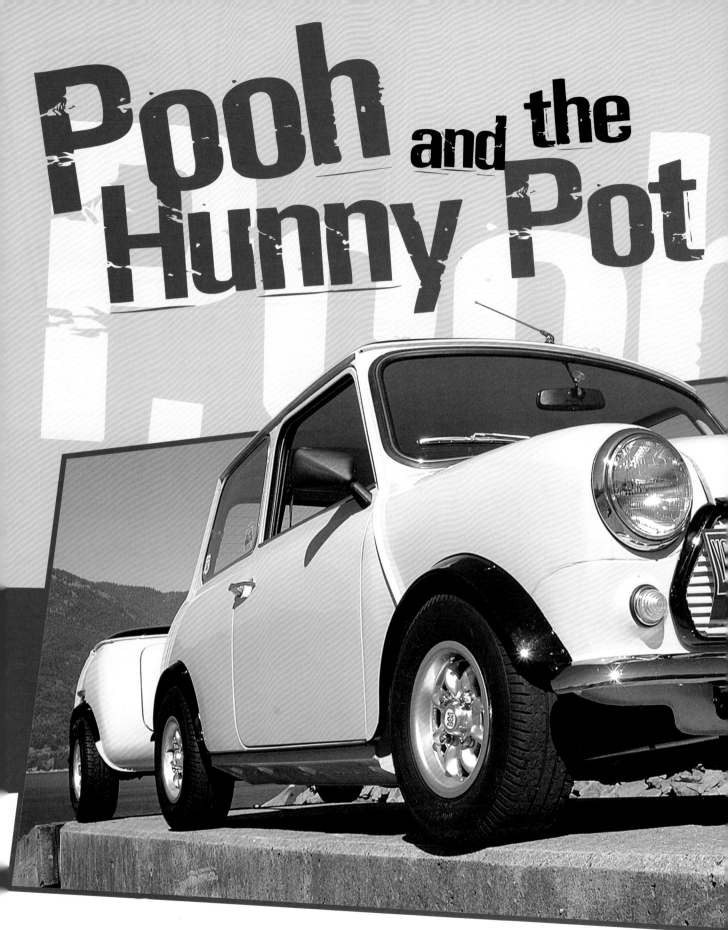

Pooh and the Hunny Pot

R ick Higgs looks and sounds entirely normal and sensible, and so does his Mini. Until you notice the trailer on the back, which is used to pack enough stuff for Rick and his wife Elaine to drive multi-thousand-mile trips around America.

Rick is a top Madman, and likes nothing better than charging around on the more interesting routes in North America. He lives in Vancouver, which is in the far north-western corner of the continent, so he has to drive thousands of miles more than people who live in the middle: it's just as well that he likes driving, then.

North America offers a lot of Mini fun, but the distances between venues are vast. For a Vancouverite to go to the Spring Thing in Florida and back is 5,600 miles: that's about the same distance as driving from London right through Europe and all of Africa to Cape Town. Pooh's first trip, 28 days after the engine was first fired up,

was to the Mini Meets on both sides of the continent, a trip of 8,000 miles plus between Vancouver, Arizona and Maryland.

Pooh came into Rick's family in 1995, having only covered 25,000 miles in its first 15 years, so the poor thing must have suffered a horrible fright when it found out how many thousands of miles of highway it would be required to drive when it got to middle age.

Rick's Mini started off as a 1979 998cc Canadian-spec Mini Sedan with huge Canadian-spec 5mph impact bumpers. Canadians traditionally hated these bumpers: as soon as they bought a Mini they would take them off and throw them away, then replace them with English-style chrome bumpers, so Canadian bumpers are actually quite rare now. Rick kept his, and recently gave them to me: as a Brit I think they're weird and cool, so they're going to be fitted to my own Canadian Mini.

Rick's car was named Pooh by his wife Elaine, because it was originally poo brown, or as BMC would have put it, Russet Brown. The 1970s saw some pretty indigestible colours in the trendy British spectrum: some of the BMC colour combinations, particularly when juxtaposed with stripy orange nylon seats, were quite emetic. Reliant really took the biscuit for kak colours, though – the entire 1970s Scimitar paint colour palette is based on human body fluids, mostly beginning with the letter p. Poo is one of the more attractive options. My own late and lamented Scimitar was Poo Brown with an interior in Babypoo velour, yum yum.

Rick's whole rig was conceived and designed for hard travelling. The mechanical base of his car is an engine powerful enough to deal with some fairly extreme temperatures and gradients. The little thermometer on the dash is a reminder of a long US road trip, with fellow Vancouverite and convoy companion John Goolevitch

↑ The Mini got the name Pooh from Rick's wife Elaine. Naturally, Pooh comes with a Hunny Pot.

← 'I've got a brilliant idea! Why don't we balance Rick's Mini up on that bit of concrete and take pictures of it?' This spectacular location is halfway up British Columbia's Sea to Sky Highway – rather like the Scottish Highlands but more so.

Pooh and the Hunny Pot 97

calling regularly from an air-conditioned Jeep 50 feet away to say 'Hey, the temperature just topped 90 degrees,' then ten minutes later to say 'Hey, it's 95 degrees now!' Yeah, thanks for that, John.

The original 998 is long gone, replaced by a 1275 A+, offset-bored to 1,380cc with a Swiftune cam and roller rockers. Ain't no substitoot for cubes, say the Americans: the Canadians concur with this approach, but they tend to recommend increasing engine capacity to achieve more torque. This is particularly important with Pooh because of its high 2.95:1 final drive ratio, chosen for civilised highway cruising. The spec on the engine tells a tale of bulletproof strength rather than frisky power, with a polished crank, balanced Metro rods and Powermax pistons all held together by Caterpillar and ARP bolts and studs. Everything that rotates is balanced, and carburation is a single HIF44 with a BDK needle. Electrical improvements include the uprated fuel pump, the switched cooling fan, and more and brighter lighting, and there is a relay box that reduces the demands placed on elderly Lucas wiring. The toughest electrical problem to solve was the side marker lamps on the trailer, which were positive-earthed LEDs. There's an oil cooler, and Rick is thinking about mounting a heater core from a

modern pickup as an additional front-mounted cooling radiator to support the custom two-core main rad.

Overall, Rick is well pleased with the engine. It achieved the anticipated power band with lots of low-down torque, it's demonstrably efficient as shown by its excellent fuel mileage, and it goes straight through British Columbia's fairly tight Aircare emissions testing every year, no bother. The differential ratio could possibly be improved to deal better with the weight of the trailer, but changing from the current high 2.95:1 ratio to the ideal 3.1:1 can happen next time the diff is disassembled.

Pooh's structure and suspension have received some beefing-up too, during the total stripdown and rebuild that started in the dead days between Christmas and New Year of 2004. The hard-mounted subframes have additional stitch-welding and gussets, the tie bars are heavy duty, the lower suspension arms are rose-jointed and poly bushes rule throughout. There's no rust left in the shell either – the kind of demands Rick makes on the car don't allow for structural weakness, so every panel in the car that showed even the faintest signs of bubbling was chopped out and replaced.

Where there's a Pooh there's inevitably a Hunny Pot, and Rick has followed an honourable Mini tradition of making trailers out of the back ends of dead Minis.

Hunny Pot the trailer represents some really original thinking. It's relatively easy to cut the back off a scrap Mini, fabricate a bar to hold a hitch, and weld plates over the front and top. However, Rick's trailer was made from the last foot or so of the back ends and roofs of *two* scrap Minis. The two Mini butts were, aptly enough, butt-welded together by Craig McGuire and finished off by John Goolevitch, who restored his rotten Mini properly and is therefore now an expert welder. Hiding the join along 6ft of butt-welding is no mean feat, although it helped that most Minis in Canada old enough to be scrapped are made out of fairly thick steel.

The frame and the leaf-sprung beam axle on the trailer were fabricated as a completely new structure rather than using the usual recycled Mini subframe, and the trailer's loaded weight with camping gear is about 380lb. This makes the whole Pooh-and-Hunny-Pot outfit around 2,500lb and 16ft long, still a couple of feet shorter and a thousand pounds lighter than most North American cars. And a lot cheaper to run as well – on its longest (8,000-mile) trip Pooh and the Hunny Pot achieved a remarkable 41.5mpg.

The bumblebee yellow and black trim job runs through the trailer as well as the car. The cost of trimming the trailer as well went over budget, but trimmer Murray

↑ Rather than a bodged Mini subframe, the trailer has its own unique custom chassis and suspension.

→ A wise man always carries a couple of spare bootlids with him. Hunny Pot is the back ends of two scrap Minis, welded together.

not only put up with being sidelined during the two years of this Mini build, but actively supported him, and now happily charges around the continent with him, camping out of the trailer and only complaining when faced with ice and snow, which don't impress her much.

When the project was finished, Pooh and the Hunny Pot won every show they went to, although the combo was never particularly intended for showing. Rick isn't particularly proud of the finish: as far as he's concerned it was simply done as it should be done. Boyd Coddington used to produce $150,000 hot rods that were built the same way and for the same intrinsic reason. If it's worth doing, it's worth doing well. The rig won First in Class at both Mini Meet East and Mini Meet West, having been driven more than 8,000 miles to get to both events, and also won a First in Class and an Honourable Mention at the Portland All-British Field Meet out of a field of 805 cars.

After several multi-thousand-mile trips it now has a few paint chips, and there was a minor mechanical sulk after a Mini Meet, involving a failed drive flange. When it came to the photo session Rick was embarrassed about the paint chips, but for a well-used fun car it still looks pretty good.

Griessel said he'd do the work free if Rick paid for the vinyl, just because he wanted it all to look just right. It certainly does, doesn't it? Both Pooh and the Hunny Pot have many happy thousands of touring miles behind and ahead of them, and the black over BMW Liquid Yellow colour scheme is designed to be safe as well as cheery – most people will see it coming. Halogen headlights also help with that, and Canadian law requires that headlights remain switched on whenever the engine is running, quite a good safety idea.

Yellow and Minis are themes that have now crossed the generation gap. Rick's son Jeremy drives a Liquid Yellow BMW Mini, and was also involved with his dad in a previous classic Mini restoration in the early '90s. Rick is also very lucky to be married to his wife Elaine, who

Tech

ENGINE – 1,275cc A+, offset-bored to 1,380cc. 1275 crank, ground, polished, balanced, with centre main strap, Caterpillar mains bolts. Resized Metro rods, balanced, ARP big end bolts. 73.5mm Powermax pistons. Swiftune SW5 cam, 1.5:1 roller rockers, Mini Spares big bore 1380 head, ARP studs and bolts, lightened and balanced flywheel. Aldon Yellow distributor with SW5 advance curve, NGK BP6ES plugs, Kingsborne leads. HIF44 with BDK needles, K&N filter with sub-stack, milled aluminium spacer, 5/16in double-filtered fuel line. Ceramic-coated Mini Spares big bore intake manifold and big bore LCB, side-exit RC40. Two-core, ¾in dimpled-tube radiator, 11-row oil cooler, electric fan.

TRANSMISSION – Orange diaphragm, standard clutch plate, A+ gears and ratios, central oil pickup. 2.95:1 final drive ratio, CWP gear set. Quickshift.

BRAKES – Cooper S uprights and discs, standard pads. Rear S drums, standard linings. Braided lines, tandem master cylinder.

SUSPENSION – Hard-mounted subframes, adjustable HD tie bars, rose-jointed lower suspension arms, adjustable camber/castor, poly bushes. Hi-Los, KYB shocks. Trailer uses dead axle, leaf springs.

WHEELS AND TYRES – Minilite 5J x 10, Yokohama A008, 165/70 x 10.

INTERIOR – Mini seats custom-upholstered, with custom door cards, visors, rear arch covers, parcel shelf, dash pad. Tacho. Door handles/winders from MGB and E-Type Jag. Pioneer 200W four-speaker sound system.

EXTERIOR – Reversion to chrome bumpers, roof drains revert to earlier style. Replaced floor, outer sills, heel board, A-panels, wings, front valance. Halogen headlamps and driving lamps, roof antenna. Black over BMW Liquid Yellow 902.

← Engine has a sting in its tail, with 1,380cc, Swiftune cam and Mini Spares big-bore head.

↓ A Mini with a trailer is unusual, but a matching Mini and trailer rig constructed with this amount of care and attention is another thing entirely.

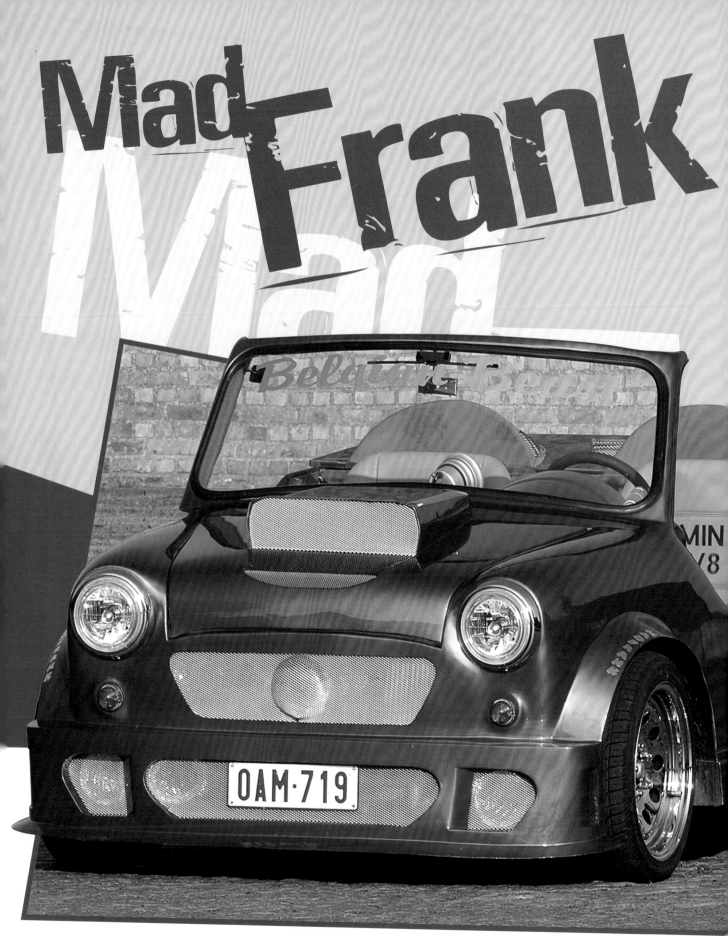

Mad Frank

I first met Zeebrugge's Mad Frank a decade ago, when he was showing his previous car, a Minivan, at the Hop Farm Mini meeting in Kent. The van was a work of art in sheet steel, and also had an immensely powerful sound system in the back that used to win sound-off competitions at shows. The system was so powerful it literally blew the roof off the van: during one competition the sound suddenly went weird and flat, and when Frank investigated he discovered that the seam between the side and roof on one side of the van had split wide open. That van also had a Perspex panel in the bonnet, and beneath that a Perspex panel let into the rocker cover through which you could see the rockers working, illuminated by little lights.

After the van, the V8 Mini was Mad Frank's next creation. His madness actually conceals much method, as he's a full-time carrossier and his Belgian Beasts are rolling advertising for him. His day job is massaging the bodywork of boring Audis and Citroëns so that they look indefinably different, but without making any identifiable changes. Belgium is firmly under the thumbs of EU penpushers,

and it's illegal to make any significant changes to TUV-approved standard vehicles. So Frank adjusts the shape of a wheel arch, drops a bonnet line by a centimetre or two, massages the door gaps, takes half a coil off the springs. If the cops stop somebody because their car looks a bit sexier than the other Euroboxes, it's hard for them to identify exactly why the car looks better.

Before the dead hand of TUV stopped the fun, there were no formal specifications for officials to use to regulate Belgian car enthusiasts, so with no written standard specs owners can do what they like with earlier cars. The V8 Mini represents Frank doing just that. His Belgian Beast is legally a 1965 Mini 850. As long as the brakes stop it and the lights light up, that's more or less all the law requires from it.

Originally he acquired a Dodge V8 out of a Dutch fire brigade pickup, laid it on his garage floor, then welded the front and back axles of a Ford Granada together with the engine in the middle. He then chopped the roof off a Mini shell, cut the roofless body in four, dropped the four bits of bodywork on top of the engine and chassis and filled in the gaps with new steel. The back end is 34cm wider than the standard Mini, but the front end, weirdly, is very slightly narrower than a standard Mini. The headrest shapes were formed by wrapping sheets of steel round a big industrial pipe. The air scoops down the side are real, and feed the rear radiator with cool air.

An interior structure was formed that allowed enough foot-room to drive the car, and when the bodywork was finished it was coated in a paint commissioned specially from Du Pont, using more flip-flop colours than had ever been used before. The engine was so big that the water-

↑ A stonking Dodge V8 is just the thing for livening up a dull Mini. Short exhausts and minimal silencing mean it sounds like a thunderstorm having a psychotic episode after somebody said it had a fat bum.

← Mad Frank's Belgian Beast is now in its second incarnation with a new chassis, new paint and new interior after another few thousand hours of work.

pump pulley stuck out through the radiator grille, so it was also painted in four-way flip-flop, and it changed colour as it revolved. Very fetching.

The radiator was relocated to the back as there wasn't even room for an ant in the engine bay. Amazing though the car looked, it handled like a farm trailer and after a few years Frank pulled the shell off, scrapped the original chassis and started again. This time he paid more attention to the geometry, and made much of his own suspension from scratch. It's not necessarily particularly elegant, but it works a lot better. Weight is not really an issue compared to the importance of strength, so the suspension components Frank has fabricated are roughly the same size as the I-beams that hold skyscrapers together … they're not going to break. The rear end is still independent but it's now designed rather than just built, and when you give the car some welly it hooks up much better than before. Obviously it will still pull an instant wheelie as soon as the tyres get a grip, but the difference now is that Frank has some idea what's going to happen

when the front end comes back down again: previously it was pretty random as to whether it would lurch to the left or the right, depending on which front wheel came down and hit the ground first.

The new interior is the result of more thought than the earlier version, and is almost entirely scratchbuilt. It was made of various wood, plastic and metal pieces, with a collection of bits of other car dashboard parts such as the vents, and then the basic shape was coated with a thick layer of GRP. The rough surface of the fibreglass was then sanded back, filled, sanded and filled until it finished up ready for paint, and ready to be fitted with an impressive collection of instruments.

The car's old paint job is now some very expensive dust on Frank's garage floor, and the new finish is a deep metallic yellow-gold candy, which involves many layers of translucent paint, each meticulously wet-sanded between coats. The deeper the colour of a candy finish, the more weeks of work have gone into the paintwork prep.

Frank's Mini is now a more tractable and comfortable

← The headrest shapes were created by wrapping sheet steel round a big pipe.

beast, and possibly even more fun that it was before. The V8 makes all the right noises, and its enormous torque means that Frank can put it in gear, lock up the front brakes and let the engine revolve the rear wheels slowly round as the car remains still. Cheaper than burnouts, and also more cool.

Cooling has always been a problem, as these huge Mopar V8s normally sit in the vast engine bay of a full-size pickup, where you could hold a dinner party for eight and still have room for a dance afterwards. Jamming one of these monsters into a tiny engine bay means that the

→ The water-pump used to stick out of the front of the car and was painted in flip-flop colours so it changed colour while spinning. It's now discreetly concealed behind a new grille.

OAM·719

← The back streets of Zeebrugge are Frank's personal racetrack. The exhaust thunder bounces off the walls, and all the babies and BMWs wail in panic.

↑ Complete new interior and dash were more or less crafted from scratch.

→ New central console carries DVD player, screen and sound system. Colour-coded instrument bezels are a nice touch.

whole engine heats up, not just the coolant. There is some air-cooling effect on the whole engine block in most cars as moving air passes through a car's engine bay, but if there's no room for air movement the engine tends to cumulatively heat up despite the efforts of the radiator. My 1990s Chevy V8-powered Cobra was dreadful for this: as soon as I saw traffic on the horizon I had to jump out of the car, open the bonnet an inch or two and rest it on the bonnet pins to provide an exit for the hot engine-bay air, or the thing would brew up big time and spit the rad hoses off. Uncool in every sense.

Frank's solution was to wrap the manifolds to shift some heat out of the engine bay, and then to jam an air-to-air turbo intercooler into a corner of the bay with the engine coolant running through that as well as the radiator. That did the job, and the cooling is now under control even when the V8 heat-sink effect gets going in traffic. The headers themselves are stumpy and short, and they don't have elegant and ideal matched primary pipes snaking towards collector boxes. You can tune engines for more torque or more bhp by adjusting the length of the primary pipes coming out of the cylinder heads, but not if you've squeezed a barrel into a pint pot and only have a couple of inches before the exhaust manifold hits the chassis. The current arrangement probably loses a few bhp off the top end as a result: well, boo-hoo. Mad Frank's Belgian Beast has enough power to be going on with.

Tech

ENGINE – Dodge V8, bored and stroked to the max. Steel crank and rods, fast road camshaft. Carter AFB four-barrel carb with B&M ram air filter. Custom wrapped headers, radiator relocated to rear, additional front intercooler in water cooling system.

TRANSMISSION – Six-speed high/low range Mopar automatic gearbox.

SUSPENSION – Front, custom-made double wishbones with coilover shocks. Rear, independent, custom setup with modified Ford suspension components.

BRAKES – Ford Granada system and solid discs all round.

WHEELS AND TYRES – American Custom Chrome with Dunlop R/T Qualifiers rear, Pirelli P5000 front.

INTERIOR – Custom GRP console and floors, Auto-Style programmable tacho with shift light, Autostyle water temp, oil pressure, voltmeter, ammeter, oil temperature, vacuum and boost gauges. JVC KD-SH707R head unit, Marquant DVD player.

EXTERIOR – Custom steel body based on original Mini panels. Orange candy paint.

↑ The original Belgian Beast was a cool all-steel Minivan that literally blew its roof off during a sound system competition: the vibration and air compression from the speakers split the gutter seam all the way along.

↓ The Beast hooks up much better with its new chassis design, and also steers better when the front wheels are touching the road.

Admirable
Nelsons

↓ With the outside temperature at a nasty 11° below zero, shooting the Turbo Woody in a heated hangar seemed a smart move.

← Rachel and Andy with most of their collection, which has since expanded.

Andy and Rachel Nelson are enthusiasts' enthusiasts: their entire lives revolve around playing with Minis. Currently they own a '64 Cooper S, '65 and '67 road sedans, a '65 Cooper racer and a BMW Mini. Not a huge number, but each Mini is gleaming perfection.

Andy is a commercial pilot, and Rachel is a manager for Harbour Air, which flies seaplanes from Vancouver BC to Victoria harbour, a short but spectacular flight carried out at 1,000ft or so over rocky little islands and beaches.

They're currently leaving Vancouver and heading for Toronto to find enough space for their Mini collection. Surely a pilot and a seaplane company executive could afford a house with a huge garage, even in expensive Vancouver? Yes, they could, but they've always spent all their money on playing with Minis and latterly on racing them, and if they stayed in Vancouver too much of their Mini budget would go on boring mortgage payments. They've already sorted out a huge Toronto workshop for the Minis. How about a Toronto house? Whatever, they'll sort one out when they get there, or just live in the workshop.

Andy was a mechanic for 12 years before becoming more ambitious and training to be a pilot, and the combination of good piloting practice and good mechanical practice has been very effective in building a string of top-class roadgoing Minis and then successful track Minis. Everything is prepared in advance and checked over thoroughly and in the correct order.

The 1965/61 Turbo Woody is a good example of a Nelson car. Andy bought it as scrap when he was 19, during his apprenticeship in a British car specialist garage. The Woody was intended to provide space for the couple's two English Bulldogs. That was in 1989, so the bulldogs were in doggy heaven way before the car was finished.

The car's engine was long gone, and the woodwork was in a pile in the back: the Woody was fast approaching scrap status, but Andy decided to bring it back from the edge with help from another dead 1961 example. The project was sidelined for years on a few occasions, and was only really finished quite recently.

The detailing inside and out is exquisite, and there is

22

← Pilots are usually nit-picky, methodical perfectionists. The live ones are, anyway. The same approach pays off when building Minis.

ENGINE – **Metro Turbo A+ 1275, bored to 1,312cc. Balanced Metro crank. MEGA turbo pistons with chrome rings. Mini Spares turbo cam, Vernier adjustable timing gearset. Sodium-cooled 29mm Turbo exhaust valves, 35mm inlet valves, Mini Spares uprated anti-coil-bind springs, 1.5:1 roller rockers. Stage 3 polished head. Avonbar/Aldon turbo distributor, Lucas coil, Pertronix electronic ignition, NGK plugs, copper leads, NGK motorcycle caps. MG Metro Turbo 1.75in HIF SU carb, with Avonbar high boost needle and dashpot spring, K&N air filter. Metro Turbo high-volume fuel pump with special regulator. Metro T3 turbocharger with 10psi wastegate actuator. Metro Turbo inlet and exhaust manifold, Maniflow downpipe and 2in Maniflow twin bore exhaust system. Estimated 120–130bhp at the wheels.**

COOLING **system – Mini Spares two-core rad with six-blade tropical fan and extra electric fan, additional rad in o/s inner wing. Sixteen-row oil cooler with twin electric fans and braided lines. ERA replica cooling duct at rear of bonnet to cool turbo area. Large-impeller water pump.**

TRANSMISSION – **Jack Knight five-speed straight-cut close-ratio, with matching drop gears. Turbo clutch, Orange diaphragm, lightweight steel flywheel and backplate. 3.4:1 final drive with four-pin diff. KAD quickshift.**

BRAKES – **Non-assisted, silicone fluid. Front, Metro Turbo 8.4in vented discs, Metro four-pot calipers, standard pads. Rear, standard cylinders and linings, Super Minifin alloy drums.**

SUSPENSION – **Hi-Los, standard rubber cones with Spax shocks. Front, 1.5° lower arms, adjustable tie bars, poly bushes. Rear, adjustable camber brackets, new subframe with aluminium tie-down plates. MkIV rack with S-type steering arms.**

WHEELS AND TYRES – **Minator 5J x 12 alloy wheels, 165/60 R12 Yokohama A510 tyres.**

INTERIOR – **Cobra Le Mans recliners in Blackrock fabric, with rear seats trimmed to match. Newton Commercial/custom trim and carpets. Driver's side Leaf six-point harness, passenger side lap-belt. Standard main dash dial with MG oil-water gauge, Auto Meter boost gauge, period Smiths tacho.**

EXTERIOR – **ERA replica bonnet scoop, Wood & Pickett front arch extensions, bulkhead modified to clear turbo. Cibie halogen headlights. Viper red paint. Window tints, Cooper grille.**

no sign of any short cuts. Replacement panels include the front and rear floors, sills, rear valance, front wings and grille panel, and numerous hand-fabricated repair sections. Paint prep on the inside rear floorpans is as good as that on the front wings, a standard that requires literally hundreds of hours of fine-grade wet and dry.

Both Rachel and Andy get stuck in – they're always out in the garage, rubbing happily away from after work to midnight, both obsessed and both happy to be fiddling about with Minis rather than watching telly or eating food or doing boring house stuff. It helps that North American TV is mostly 200 channels of crap, so it's not tempting even if you're tired.

I suppose the Turbo Woody is a bit mad. It has the performance of a serious nutter Mini, but it still looks like a gleaming half-timbered estate car, which would normally have a picnic basket, some prize plaques and some polish in the back rather than a can of race fuel. The body is visually standard apart from the scoop and the wheel arches, although there have been some bulkhead mods to make room for the turbo.

When Rachel invited me to try this car out, I was in there like a rat up a drainpipe. Do I like playing with turbo Minis? Do bears poo in the woods? After a few years living in Canada I can confirm that bears do indeed poo in the woods on a regular basis, and cheerfully mix their metaphors as well.

The first thing that grabs you about this car is how unexpectedly fast it is, and the second is how smooth. Turbo Minis don't usually feature subtle power curves – mostly it's nothing much, nothing much, nothing much, *blam*. This one gave nice silky smooth punch up to 7,000, and the

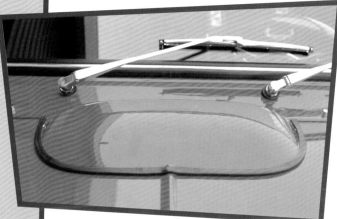

⬆ Reverse scoop as fitted to ERA turbo Minis doesn't spoil the car's looks, and helps to keep engine bay temperatures down.

➜ Racing cars with gleaming show-condition engine bays actually do go faster: it means the whole car has been built to this standard.

fifth gear allows for civilised cruising, apart from the noise. A whining Mini gearbox is either knackered or it has seriously trick guts in it, and this one turned out to be a straight-cut five-speed Jack Knight number. I've been hearing recently that slant-cut gears work just as well as straight-cut, but if you've paid as much for your gearbox as some people pay for their entire car, it's nice to hear the straight-cut whine to remind you that you're getting value for money. There's also the funky *pllfffff* noise from the dump valve on the turbo, so the soundtrack is pretty cool; there's no sound system in the car at all, as the in-car entertainment is all provided by what goes on under the bonnet.

The little replica ERA backwards turbo scoop is the only outward sign that the car has been radically interfered with, so it's top fun on the street if you come across somebody at the traffic lights who previously thought they had a fast car.

The engine started off as a Metro Turbo unit, but was inevitably beefed up. It's balanced throughout, and with its light steel flywheel and turbo it whips up to 7,000 no bother. It all went together very well, with a few hairy moments while fitting the ultra-hard chrome piston rings: they can only be bent open a small amount before they snap. The engine has been completely reliable, and with the boost at a reasonable 10lb and good balancing there's no reason why it shouldn't keep going for a long time.

The list of engine mods is pretty hardcore but not too extreme, so the car is still usable in the city as well. The power band is wide and the original flat spot at zero boost was sorted out by Avonbar turbo carb mods. There are enough gears and enough power to allow quite serious track speeds, so the Yokos and the decent brakes are used to their full capacity.

The comprehensive cooling system is designed to deal with track use in a hot Canadian summer. There are in total four fans, two water radiators and one oil radiator. For autocrossing between cones on hot summer airfields, this is great, because everything stays cooler than Clint Eastwood. On an uncharacteristically freezing Vancouver day with the wind chill at the airport taking the temperature down to -11°, the engine is so well cooled it still needs the choke after it's been idling for 20 minutes.

Brakes are 8.4in vented discs rather than the original feeble drums, and the suspension has also been upgraded with Hi-Los, poly bushes, 1.5° lower arms, adjustable tie bars and whatever other subtle and barely visible improvements were available.

↖↑ All the Nelsons' cars, race or road, look better than new. Everything is squeaky clean and sorted to perfection before it goes in.

↑ Five minutes before the race, and Andy is relaxed and ready. A 7-litre Cobra and a 5-litre Tiger don't know they're about to be humiliated by a 1.3-litre Mini.

The longer wheelbase may also give the car more of a performance edge over a Mini saloon on corners due to the extra stability of the longer wheelbase, but I have to admit that pushing a Woody to the limit isn't a concept that had crossed my mind before I found myself looning around in this car. Sorry, conducting a sober professional journalistic evaluation of it.

The Turbo Woody was around for a while, but it attracted the attention of somebody who had enough taste to realise how fab the car was, and who also had enough money to make an unrefusable offer for it. The Nelsons were getting seriously stuck into vintage racing at the time, which is more expensive than a Keith Richards drug regime and just as addictive, so they took the offer, and the money went straight into the next racing Mini.

A high point of the Nelsons' vintage racing career so far has been the 2006 Rolex Monterey Historic Automobile Races. A few Mini-Coopers were grudgingly tolerated at this posh and expensive event, but only because Cooper racing cars were the featured marque. That's proper Cooper single-seaters, you understand, not our low-rent Cooper-badged BMC Minis. Minis will probably never be invited again.

Ironically, the Americans failed to understand that Minis were and are among the very few completely classless cars you can buy. Mother's cleaning lady had one, Mother had one and so did many British aristos, who wouldn't have owned anything as vulgar as an American car. Or a Rolex, come to think of it.

The thought of driving a Mini at the Monterey Historics appealed big-time to Andy and Rachel. They needed a Cooper with racing papers for the event, and tracked down a '65 Cooper S that had been raced from new. After 30 years of being either raced or neglected, it was nasty enough to present a worthwhile challenge even to the intrepid Nelsons. There wasn't much rust, but there had been a few rugby-style incidents on the track, and the car had been both rolled over and heavily thumped in the right rear quarter.

They removed the roof, then the rear quarter, then scraped the whole shell down to bare metal and rust. Where possible the original panels were saved. Dents and rust were hammered out and cut out, and the fuel cell was sealed in the boot. US vintage racing requires originality apart from safety mods, and the Nelsons were happy to comply, leaving the S as original as possible.

The car was resprayed at home. Hundreds of hours were spent on perfect prep, then lots and lots of paint was sprayed and laboriously cut back to a gleaming finish.

The Monterey rules require a full interior, so although the driver's seat is a racing shell, it's been trimmed in the same colours and material as the rest of the Newton Commercial replica interior.

The engine build proceeded at the same measured pace as the body, so when one of the cam bearings turned out to be conical rather than tubular, there was time to replace it. The engine is genuinely A-series with as much development and strengthening as the spirit of the rules will allow. The intention was to build the optimum racing Mini engine – fast enough and strong enough. A delicate balance. The original crank had come out in several pieces, illustrating just that point. The new crank was wedged, balanced, cross-drilled and nitrided. The rods remain S, but well worked over – lightened, balanced, polished and held together with ARP bolts.

The head is a Longman GT14, much ported and polished, with big 37mm intake valves and standard 29mm exhausts. It's shaved to create 16.5cc combustion chambers with a compression ratio of 12.2:1, so it's just as well the crank is uprated. The AEG 649 cam's timing was perfected with a Swiftune alloy-centred vernier cam gear adjuster.

There are some nice details – the original S rockers were shaved and lightened to cut unnecessary reciprocating weight, and they run with light brass spacers separating them. Reliable sparks were also very important: if the engine splutters when you floor it on the track, you might as well be running an 850. The Cooper S distributor was retained, but fitted with lighter springs to speed up the ignition advance, and Pertronix were brought in when it came to the actual sparks.

Proper cooling for Monterey was crucial: the circuit is inland from the California coast, and the weather can get pretty hot. A double rad is cooled by a plastic multiblade fan and an uprated water pump, and a damaged piece of original inner wing in front of the fan was trimmed off and left off for more airflow. Just to be sure, a 13-row oil cooler was added as well – hot oil is good, but boiling oil is bad: just ask a medieval castle-besieger's ghost.

The suspension remains hydrolastic, which is unusual for racing. However, Andy has found that with a controller to adjust pressure back to front and with a factory rear anti-roll bar, it all works very well. Corners are taken on three wheels anyway, so keeping the car smooth enough for him to be able to keep his feet on the pedals may be a very smart move.

GBA 688 made Mini history first time out after its rebuild, and performed faultlessly. Andy rather tactlessly beat two Shelby Cobras, a Lotus Seven, a Ginetta, an Alfa Romeo and a Sunbeam Tiger. That'll make sure Minis are never invited back to the Rolex Monterey Historics.

To keep up with their future exploits check out Andy and Rachel's website at www.arperformance.citymax.com.

ENGINE – 1275S, now 1,293cc. Rotating assembly balanced. EN40B wedged, cross-drilled, nitrided crank. S rods, lightened, polished, ARP bolts. AE Mega pistons, chrome top rings. Swiftune alloy-centred Vernier adjuster on an AEG 649 cam. Longman GT14 ported, polished race head shaved to 16.5cc combustion chambers, 12.2:1 compression, 37mm inlet valves, 29mm exhaust valves. Pertronix ignition. S distributor with light advance springs. NGK BP8ES plugs, Bumblebee motorcycle leads. Generic alloy inlet manifold, 2 x 1.5in SU with Keith Calver ITG filter. LCB Maniflow, RC40 centre exit exhaust. Mini Spares two-core radiator with multi-blade fan, oversize water pump pulley, oversize water impeller, 13-row oil cooler. Holley Red 97GPH fuel pump, low pressure regulator.

TRANSMISSION – Ultralight steel flywheel, AP bonded race/rally clutch, orange spot diaphragm; three-synchro straight-cut gears, EVO straight-cut drop gears, roller bearing idle, central oil pickup.

SUSPENSION – Hydrolastic, stock hydro return springs, adjustable front/back bias valve, Koni shocks, factory rear anti-roll bar, upgraded bushes throughout.

BRAKES – 7.5in Cooper discs, Porterfield carbon metallic pads, Cooper S drums rear.

WHEELS AND TYRES – 5J x 10 Minilite alloys, with Hoosier TD165/70 x 10 vintage-racing bias-belted (crossplies).

INTERIOR – Cobra racing seat trimmed to match Newton Commercial replica interior, five-point harness, eight-point custom TIG welded rollcage; period aftermarket gear lever extension, headlining signed by Michael Cooper, grippy pedal pads, oil/water combo gauge, oil temp gauge.

EXTERIOR – New roof, rear quarter and front end panels, RH sills, Old English White with black roof.

← The race Mini's engine performed perfectly. Luck is involved as well, though: Rachel's engine was equally well prepared, and ran beautifully until it threw a rod through the crankcase.

Z-Cars

↓ This steel-bodied Z-Cars Mini looks innocent enough: in fact it could still pass for a stock Mini.

Chris Allanson, boss of Z-Cars, is one of Britain's top kit car madmen. He's an ex-cop who's old enough to remember the grainy 1960s black-and-white television series *Z-Cars*, which was rather fab. Lots of Ford Zephyrs with fins screeching around, and Brian Blessed's shouting-based acting career was launched. The crims used to say 'It's a fair cop, guv,' when caught bang to rights, and the traffic police didn't have to wear stab vests. Z-Cars is a top name for Chris's company, then.

Chris no longer charges around in cop cars, he charges around in his own cars. He tried to scare the hell out of me but failed. It's not that I'm particularly brave: I'm not. Too much imagination, and I enjoy being alive. However, I've been writing about fast cars for 20 years now and experience tells me when I should be scared. Inexperienced and overconfident young drivers in fast production cars with no rollover bars scare me, drunks in pickups scare me, but Chris doesn't.

He makes a good effort, of course, and takes me out on his regular scary route at mad speeds. This works very well at terrifying and impressing customers: he scared the poo out of my brother, who now wants a Z-Cars Mini.

The company's impressively big and clean premises is situated on farmland on the remote coastline of Yorkshire (which has to mean very low overheads and a good chance of surviving recessions: Chris may be mad but he's not daft).

The tiny local roads are empty. It's wet, and Chris fires up a Honda-powered Z-Mini with a crackle from the exhaust. He potters out of the workshop on to his long,

splashy private driveway and floors it. The engine howls, we hit the seat backs, and after a few engine screams and gearchanges he's heading for a T-junction at about 100mph on a ten-foot-wide wet surface and it looks like we're heading for a very big accident. However, no worries. Chris used to hold the world road-car record for 0–60mph in a twin-engined Tiger kit car; he currently races a very nasty Z-Mini; the car we're in has huge brakes and a substantial rollcage; there's only a shallow ditch and a field beyond the junction; and he knows every inch of this road in all conditions. We slam into the straps as the brakes bite, and I just enjoy the ride. I keep a grip on the harness, just in case he hits some diesel or something and a ditch flips the car, because in a rollover you don't want your arm getting outside the car if the door or window comes off. There's not much margin for error here, as Chris is probably going quite close to too fast. Out on the public road, and he doesn't even have to break the speed limit on his little terror tour: taking a 20mph corner at 60mph makes his point very effectively.

Most people aren't used to cars and drivers like this, so they scream in terror for the first few corners, then begin to scream with excitement from the visceral thrill of it, and by the time the demo drive is over they're gagging to buy a kit.

And so they should, because these things are very fine toys.

Some of them are still basically Minis, with either bike engines or Honda engines in the back. The Mini normally weighs around 1,500lb, and used to win rallies with a 65bhp 1,275cc engine. In fact, most of us are aware that in the

23

← Chain drive goes from the bike gearbox to the diff. The visible starter motor is actually the electric backup motor.

→ 160bhp+ and rear-wheel drive reminds you that FWD is only good for packaging and cost savings. The Honda B-series Civic engine is top fun in Minis, but double the fun if you put it in the back.

← Even the BUSA lettering on the back won't mean much to most people.

↓ The rollcage is part of the structure, but you can stick with a more traditional dash if the digital variety doesn't suit you.

↘ The Honda car is naughtier than the posh red ZBusa, with visible air intakes and outlets. Racetrack sound level rules are now tougher than noise regulations for street cars, as bureaucrats achieve tighter control. You would not believe how fast this thing goes, and it's not even blown or turbocharged.

Monte Carlo rally, Mini Coopers wiped the floor with the French so brutally that they had to cheat and disqualify the Minis for incorrectly-switched headlights to get a French car into the top ten.

So take this 1,500lb go-kart and fit it with a 225bhp Honda Vtec Type R engine and it's now three and half times as powerful. If you want it even more exciting, fit a blown Hayabusa engine.

But that's the slow version of the Z-Car Mini. A faster Z-Car, but still a regular roadgoing production vehicle, now beats the old world-record 3.15-second time with an incredible 2.6 seconds, and 5.7 seconds to 100mph. 2.6 seconds is Formula One acceleration, leaving pedestrian McLarens struggling at 3.2 seconds and donkey-cart Ferrari 360s and geriatric Shelby 427 Cobras crawling along way behind at 4.6 seconds.

The faster Z-Car Monte Carlo option is a spaceframe with a fibreglass hat on it. It's 30% lighter than a standard Mini at 1,000lb, retaining the unbeatable handling, and something like seven times as powerful for its weight as the cars that humiliated the French in a world-class rally.

I tried two Z-Car types. The first was a steel Mini, owned by the boss of the doomed Rover group, and was still very much a Mini, but instead of the cute but wheezy 1,275cc A-series it had a 1,300cc Suzuki Hayabusa engine in the back. Only the cubic capacity is the same: rather than a plodding cast-iron shopping engine, the Hayabusa motor is a manic superbike screamer with a redline in five figures and power options from 160bhp to 400bhp. The Hayabusa engine and box doesn't weigh much and is in any case mounted in the perfect mid-rear position for weight-transfer-induced rear wheel loading and

maximum grip. The chain from the bike engine goes to a diff and then to the road via independent suspension and driveshafts. The rear seats, floor and subframe of the Mini are filleted and replaced by the Z-Cars custom frame that mounts the engine and suspension. The outer shell of the Mini remains intact, as does everything from the B-pillars forwards, although the engine bay is obviously just used for the fuel tank and radiators. So one of the cool things about retaining the Mini shell is the sleeper aspect: you can wave cheerily to a Porsche or Ferrari driver at the traffic lights and then humiliate them at will, driving a cute little Mini. How cool is that?

It may strike you that superbikes have no reverse gear: this is taken care of by a starter motor attached to the

Tech
Steel Z-Cars Mini

ENGINES – Bike engines: Yamaha R1, Suzuki GSXR1000 or Suzuki Hayabusa. Car engines: 2-litre Honda Civic Type, or other 1,600cc/1,800cc B-series.

TRANSMISSION – For bike engines, six-speed sequential with electric reverse; for car engines, standard Honda five-speed.

SUSPENSION – Front, adjustable double wishbones, rose-joints, Protech adjustable inboard coilover shocks. Rear, independent fully adjustable multilink, Protech coilover shocks.

BRAKES – Various options, rear discs and calipers supplied.

WHEELS AND TYRES – 13in and larger, as Mini rear trailing arm wheel size restriction is removed.

KIT components – Fully assembled roll cage/subframe, rear disks and calipers, gear lever and cable, fuel tank, radiator and mounts, front subframe. Options include aluminium firewalls, limited slip diff, electric reverse, 200 more bhp, brake upgrades, etc.

WEIGHT – With Hayabusa, 1,268lb. With Honda, 1,433lb.

↑ The Monte Carlo is also available with either Honda or bike power. This one has Yamaha R1 power.

↓ ↘ This is really a street-legal racing spaceframe that wears a Mini-shaped hat.

chain wheel. You just press a button to back up.

This rear-bike-engine format when applied to a steel Mini is still a usable daily car, if you use enough soundproofing and carpeting to muffle the shriek of the engine, but the 'busa motor at 1,300cc has enough cubes and thus enough torque to cruise well at lower revs, unlike some smaller bike engines that have to be screaming their plums off at 10,000rpm before you get any power out of them. The engine's efficiency also gives good gas mileage if you can keep your foot out of it. Other advantages of the rear-mid-engine configuration include better general balance, better brake balance and stopping power, and, of

course, no Mini-style torque steer, as the front wheels are just used for steering and braking.

The more extreme Z-cars Monte Carlo model almost completely disposes of the Mini: it retains the paperwork, glasshouse, lights and a 2in lowered Mini visual silhouette, but that's about all. There's a rear-mounted bike engine or a Honda Type R engine, a spaceframe rollcage, an aluminium floor and some GRP Mini-lookalike panels. The wheels stick out a foot on either side, so the grip is phenomenal. Power to weight ratio is between 250bhp/ton and 600bhp+/ton with a still-streetable Hayabusa engine. These are the Z-Cars with sub-three second

0–60 times that would keep up with Michael Schumacher in a full Formula One car until air resistance slowed them or Schumacher rammed them.

You can pick'n'mix too, of course – and you can get Z-cars to change things and make things for you, at a rate of £40 an hour. In the big workshop there's a TVR with a Nissan Skyline 4WD drivetrain, there's a Citroën 2CV that's been Zedded with a spaceframe and a bike engine, and there's a BMW 'Mini' with a decent engine in it, a tuned Vtec out of a Honda rather than the original shrunken Dodge Neon device.

Most of Z-Cars' business will continue to be mad Minis, and their level of expertise and professionalism accelerates as fast as the cars – the steel-Mini build manual is on DVD and available from Z-Cars or from the producer www.Minifilms.co.uk, who also have other interesting Mini film material.

The build DVD is excellent and comprehensive, and not only tells you everything you could want to know but includes some top footage of Z-Cars on the track.

These are not cheap kits, but you get what you pay for, and the quality of the engineering is obvious. Given their genuine supercar performance, they cost peanuts. A Bugatti Veyron will match a Z-Cars Monte Carlo's performance, but it costs $1.7 million and needs every last one of its 1,001bhp to keep up.

Check out the Z-Cars website at www.zcars.org.uk or type 'YouTube Z cars' into Google if you want to see them in action. If that last sentence is gibberish, find a ten-year-old and ask them to help. Turn the speaker volume right up to get the full effect.

Tech
Z-Cars Monte Carlo

ENGINES – Bike engines: Yamaha R1, Suzuki GSXR1000 or Suzuki Hayabusa. Car engines: 2-litre Honda Civic Type, or other 1,600cc/1,800cc B-series.

TRANSMISSION – Bike engines, six-speed sequential with electric reverse; car engines, standard Honda five-speed.

SUSPENSION – Front, adjustable double A-arms, Protech coilover shocks, custom steel uprights, optional sway bar. Rear, adjustable multi-link trailing arms, Protech coilover shocks, optional sway bar.

BRAKES – Wilwood bias control, custom pendulum pedals. Front, Wilwood four-pot calipers, 235mm vented discs. Rear, Sierra Cosworth 235mm calipers/discs.

WHEELS AND TYRES – Front, 8 x 13 alloys, 195/50R13 Avon ACB10. Rear, 10 x 13 with 245/45 x 13 Avon ACB10.

KIT components – Full spaceframe, 38mm and 45mm CDS round tube steel. (FIA spec optional.) GRP body with detachable rear end. Otherwise similar to steel car.

WEIGHT – With Vtec, 1,111lb. With Hayabusa, 1,023lb.

← The yellow Monte is powered by Honda's Vtec, which is both reliable and frisky in Type R form.

Ice Racing

⬇ Nolan's Mini may look like an abandoned wreck, but it's just resting before next season.

Nolan Kitchener seems like a nice, sane, sensible bloke. He runs Cedar Valley Alignment in Mission, British Columbia. I've never heard him swear, or say anything unpleasant about anyone. However, if you take a quick look at the state of his ice racer, it doesn't look as though it's used for friendly and polite competition, does it? Ice racing is quite far along the mad scale, although being Canadian it's all organised and licensed madness, with rules.

There are very different climates in different parts of BC. The Vancouver area's climate is relatively balmy, and quite British apart from having about 60% more sunshine. I think of it as Baja Canada, and the reasonable winters and very pleasant summers are two of the good reasons why I live here. There's usually a week or two of snow annually, during which many shiny pickups fall into ditches and Hondas are scattered sideways across the roads. Snow is infrequent enough that nobody knows how to drive on it, just as in the UK.

However, start heading northwards into the interior and the picture rapidly changes. Away from the Pacific coast, quite a lot of BC has a continental climate, which tends to mean almost desert conditions, with 35° heat in the summer; but for the entire winter the temperature can remain below freezing.

Barnes Lake is a top ice-racing venue, and every winter the ice racers just wait until the lake water has frozen thick enough to carry the weight of a few dozen charging cars, and then they get on with the fun.

Although the cars tend to look disreputable, this is proper FIA-sanctioned racing, with safety rules and a code of conduct: you have to obtain a specific ice-racing licence. There's no boozing allowed, and no contamination of the ice by engine oil or antifreeze. Make a mess by tearing a driveshaft out and you have to clean it up.

Ice racing is not a free-for-all either. There's a formal one-kilometre circuit with corner marshals, and although a certain amount of automotive rugby is tolerated, this isn't banger racing.

Canadians tend to play hard when it comes to their sports, to relieve the tensions caused by being so nice all the time. Ice hockey is a good example – if you bash somebody on the head with your hockey stick, that's known as 'roughing' and is fine. If you rip his helmet off

← It's a good idea to have big brake lights to penetrate the blizzard of ice and snow your rear wheels kick up.

24

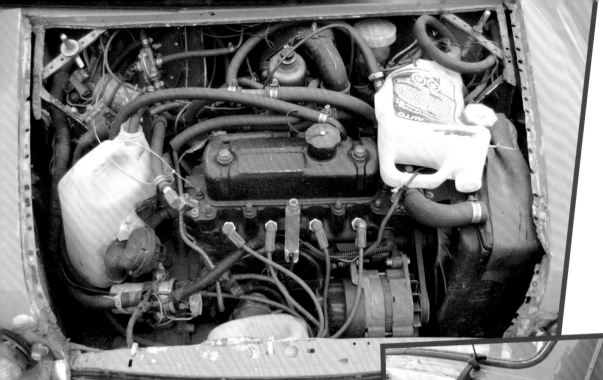

← Nolan's engine is a turbocharged 1275 – functional rather than concours. The big plastic bottle is an oil catch tank, the smaller one covers the air intake to reduce the amount of ice spray that gets sucked into the engine.

→ Studded wheels have a tendency to shred bodywork if there's any contact.

→ The interior features a full rollcage, a tatty old racing seat and a large second modern heater to supplement the Mini system.

and them bash him on the head with your stick, that's a foul and is not encouraged. You have to go pretty berserk to get into trouble, although a Vancouver Canucks player managed it recently by jumping on a guy from behind at full speed and breaking his neck. That was a going a bit far, everybody thought.

There's a parallel in Britain: go and see some Citroën 2CV racing, I strongly recommend it. 2CVs are driven by vicars and social workers who wear wholemeal pullovers and shoes that look like Cornish pasties, and because they have to be sympathetic, warm and fluffy 99% of the time, they go barking mad when they get out on the track in 2CVs. It's literally death and glory, because even the best rollcage in the world is useless if it's attached to something flimsier than a biscuit tin. Some drivers don't survive big crashes such as being T-boned at the bottom of a hill by one of the other 40 hurtling biscuit tins in the race.

Anyway, Minis are smaller and much stronger – Nolan's ice racer has already survived eight seasons. Like all ice-racing cars, it's fitted with a race-legal FIA rollcage, a full harness, fire extinguishers and tow hooks. The survival of this car for eight years is remarkable, because the mechanical stresses in ice racing are very high even if you don't get bumped on a corner and go flying up the banking and off the track. You'd think ice racing was like Speedway bikes or drifting, a matter of controlled sliding around the corners. But far from it. Novices run on studded street tyres, which are quite grippy but can be drifted on, and the more ambitious ice-racing classes run on seriously grippy tyres they have to make themselves. They glue an extra tread on to an existing tyre, just like a remould. But before the new tread is heat-glued or Vulcanised on to the tyre carcass, dozens of holes are drilled in the new tread cap and long-shanked pop rivets are inserted through the holes from behind. Then wood screws are driven into the tops of the rivets. 10in tyres that you can fit studs to are hard to find, as are directional 10in winter tyres.

So old Mini tyres with screwed recaps is what they race on, and their grip on the ice is better than a sticky Yokohama on a tarmac track: suspension, driveline and driver take quite a pounding. The reason for the bodywork looking a bit shredded is that occasionally it gets a scrape from one of these lethal studded tyres: you can see the results.

⬇Nolan's Mini hurtling across a frozen lake in northern BC during a race. The Mini still does well against more modern vehicles.

➡Nolan makes his own studded tyres with remould treads, rivets and screws.

Tech

ENGINE – Turbocharged Metro 1275 A+, bored +040. Austin America rods drilled for oil splash on piston bottoms. ARP rod bolts. Hepolite thick-crown Turbo pistons. Cam, one-off Colt Cams regrind for turbo engine. Head, fully ported, large intake valves, 1.7:1 ratio aluminium roller rockers, Isky high-lift springs, ARP head bolts. Garret turbocharger. SU sealed turbo carb with BBC needle, custom turbo distributor, manifold heating disconnected for colder air-fuel mixture, dual radiators. Power 100bhp+.

TRANSMISSION – Standard, with welded diff, 3.76:1 or 4.13:1 depending on circuit. CVs and driveshafts are regarded as disposable.

BRAKES – Standard drums. No, really. Braking is for wimps.

SUSPENSION – Fully adjustable for height, camber, toe-in and caster. Hi-Los, Spax springs and shocks.

WHEELS AND TYRES – Steel Mini wheels, tyres are recapped 145 x 10 with ¼ hex head screw into a pop rivet in the tread, or a 16mm truck stud in the tyre.

INTERIOR – One elderly racing seat, full rollcage, fire system, five-point race harness, additional heater.

Mini Limo

Jan Harde's life changed dramatically for the worse when he was involved in a crash and got his back broken — so he redressed the karmic balance by buying, dismantling, rebuilding and customising his Mini Limo. This has gone a long way towards making him feel better, because he's had an enormous amount of fun out of it and still does on a daily basis. It can't help but cheer you up when many people grin in delight as you drive past.

Jan also owns a seriously nice 1970s Mercedes convertible, but Los Angeles is full of nice open Mercs, whereas they have only one Mini Limousine. What makes the Mini Limo even more delightful is that Hollywood is crawling with seriously huge stretch limos, some based on American saloons and some now based on chopped-up obese pimp jeeps such as Cadillac Escalades, and some even based on Hummers. I mean the fake chromed Hummer lookey-likeys on Chevy Suburban chassis, not

the real army ones. Fake Hummers have to be the gayest vehicle in the world: they remind me of studded black leather posing pouches.

The drivers of the LA big boys' limos, naturally enough, scowl at the Mini Limo because its very existence takes the piss, and these people take themselves seriously. They charge a hundred bucks each to take 300lb hillbillies (actually, it's polite to say 'Appalachian-Americans' these days rather than hillbillies or rednecks) from Cow Ass, Tennessee, on a tour of the Stars' Homes, although most of that's probably bollocks: they can just point at any high wall in Beverley Hills with security cameras on it and say 'That's George Clooney's house.' Who's going to argue?

The Mini was originally built in the UK a while back by Lindsay Hayes, who took the safety and structural aspects of the project very seriously and welded in a set of beams along the sills, which make the Mini far stronger than most railway carriages. There was probably no need for such extensive strengthening, as the final car is only about as long as a Mondeo, but it's nice to know that you're riding round in something that would dent a Chieftain tank. The long wheelbase and the stiff chassis also improve the ride: it's still a Mini, but when you're riding in the front seats it doesn't feel bouncy and lively the way Minis usually do. The LA freeways are rather like the M11 but worse — they're just slabs of cracked concrete loosely laid in a general north-south direction, and in anything but a Cadillac you get a constant *badump badump* as you crash from slab to slab. Minis go *badumpbadumpbadumpbadump*; but the Mini Limo goes *badump badump badump*, which is much better.

A total of three scrap Minis were chopped up to provide all the bodywork for the Limo, and the square rear door windows had to be specially cut: the window frames can be welded together from two sets, but not

← Making a Mini Limo look right is no easy task, as the body both droops and narrows quite dramatically towards the tail: just adding a slice of dead Mini isn't enough.

↓ The office is very nice, with most of the electrics and dash guts from a 2000 Rover. Fat speakers, two of fourteen, make a fat noise.

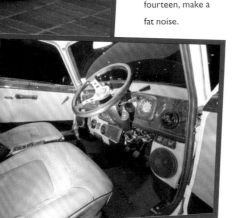

↑ Rear windows are not just tinted, but electrically operated — a Mini first?

25

the glass. A Limo is not just a Mini chopped in half with an extra bit bunged in the middle. There's a lot more to it than that.

Riding in the back is a whole different world from joining Jan in the office up front. He could have gone for the whole Hollywood pimp look with pink feather boas and Hummer chrome, but has restrained himself to a colour scheme of grey Connolly leather, walnut fittings and deep Wilton carpeting decorated with white sheepskin rugs. The centrepiece of the rear compartment is the drinks table with clinking crystal champagne flutes and a bottle of Moët et Chandon on ice.

It's just occurred to me that this has to be one of the top seduction machines ever. From experience, Ferrari Testarossas are a waste of time, but small cute cars do

blow up female frocks a bit, and if you can't work any magic in a tiny limo with *Casablanca* on the video screens, a bit of cheek and a bottle of Moët, something's far wrong with your mojo. The Mini Limo is also unique among Minis in that making lurve in it is possible without risking a visit to the chiropractor afterwards. However, I digress. As Gorgeous Wife had been left behind in Canada, all I did was ride around in the back waving at the public as they jumped up and down, pointing and squealing with delight.

Jan rather modestly says he's only put a thousand hours in to the Mini Limo, and that has been largely in getting it exactly the way he wants it. Working on the car comes at a cost for him, though – after a few operations he still has to chew morphine sticks when his back gives him a hard time, so there's a limit to how much he can achieve. He can't exactly go clambering about like a monkey and has to think strategically before doing something to the car. Fortunately he didn't get any grief at all from his wife Cathy for spending so much time fiddling with the car – if he's happy, she's happy.

The audio and cinema system is pretty impressive, with a beefy pair of pre-amps and amps, surround sound and a total of 14 speakers, so you get every nuance of *The Italian Job*. 'You're only supposed to blow the bloody doors off!'

If you wanted to do the Hollywood film cliché thing of driving through, er, Hollywood, standing up and poking out of the Limo roof with a lush filmy soundtrack belting out of the 14 speakers as your hair blows in the slipstream, you could do it: but it would be best to be a woman, young, and not bald. The Mini Limo is fully equipped for this sort of sunroof cliché action, with a Webasto sliding roof above the rear cabin, and if you want less of a breeze you can slide the roof shut and open the side windows – by pressing a button, as they're electrically operated. Have to admit the lecky rear side windows are an impressive bit of bling, although they do rather stray from the Issigonis function-and-form concept. For yet more cooling breeze, there's air conditioning front and rear.

The original engine wasn't up to hauling this sort of weight around as well as powering the air conditioning compressor, so it was replaced with the current 1,430cc MED motor, which is well capable of keeping up with the traffic. In Hollywood the traffic cruises, but on the LA interstate highways they do give it some stick. Ten lanes of Appalachian-Americans in pickups wearing wifebeater vests, and estate agents in cheap suits and BMWs, all hurtling along at 80mph and more, when they're not jammed solid in sweaty M25-style gridlock. The cops just come by to clear up the crashes, rather than trying to impose any speed limit.

Jan has just fitted a five-speed gearbox to get the

noise level down to Limo rather than Mini levels, and also because the engine will last longer at more reasonable revs. It has enough bhp to charge around a bit, but the 1,430cc capacity gives it enough torque to make good use of a fifth gear.

The major donor Mini was a 1969 Mini 1000, which had a beans-on-toast electrical system, compared to the *estouffade haricots blancs frais à l'occitane* wiring demanded by the Mini's current electrical and electronic bean-feast. Most of the electrical system was harvested from a 2000 Rover Mini, and it works pretty well most of the time, although the ghost of Joseph Lucas does occasionally haunt it, as it does most Minis – during our shoot the lighting fuse declined to pop and referred all the current to the light-switch instead, which resigned in a puff of rather worrying smoke. Such is Mini life, however, and the hazard lights still worked so no worries.

Jan wanted to achieve the ultimate luxury Mini, and I reckon he's probably done it. If anybody knows of a posher one, let me know.

Many thanks to the friendly, helpful and patient Woodland Hills Marriott staff, for the use of their forecourt for the shoot.

← Here's the money shot. There's Connolly-leathered and Wilton-carpeted room for two in comfort, with a cooled bottle of Moët in the ice bucket and *Casablanca* on the DVD screen.

ENGINE – MED 1,430cc based on 1275, polished and ported head, belt-driven MD276 cam, Aldon Yellow distributor, Metro Turbo cast plenum chamber with single SU 1.75in HIF, Range Rover VO air filter with Saab 900 fuel filler pipe used as intake tube, twin lower steady bars, custom upper steady bars, custom street-rod chromed alternator to power air conditioning system. 2000 model year electrical system. Radex aluminium racing radiator. 13-row oil cooler. Electric cooling fans. Estimated 115bhp at the crank.

TRANSMISSION – Mini Sport five-speed, Saab gear lever.

BRAKES – Stainless braided hoses, servo, DOT 5 fluid, four-pot calipers, drilled and vented discs.

SUSPENSION – Hi-Los all round, Gaz adjustable shocks over coil springs.

WHEELS AND TYRES – Minilite 6J x 12 with Yokohama A539, 165/60 x 12.

INTERIOR – Connolly leather seating, Mini Mania wheel, walnut dash and console with six gauges, Saab gear lever, Wilton carpets with sheepskin rugs. Electrically operated rear windows, champagne cooler.

EXTERIOR – Main conversion by Lindsay Hayes in UK. Three Mini bodies were used, with significant side and floor bracing steel beams. New roof paint is deep purple candy with 24-carat gold flakes. Webasto sunroof at rear.

ICE – Extreme Audio 800W system with dual pre-amps and amps, surround sound with 14 speakers, three video screens, Alpine ten-disc CD changer, in-dash Phillips Carin GPS.

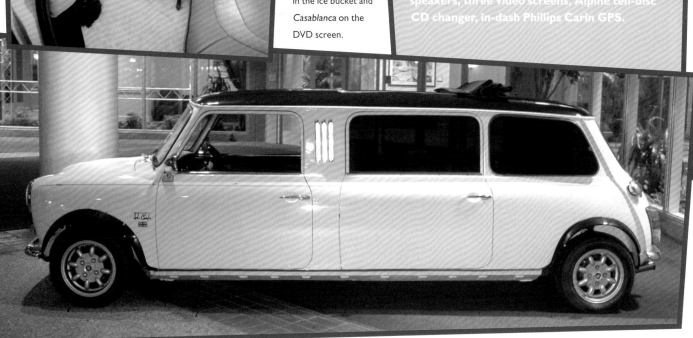

Mini Marcos

↑ The front end of the Mini Marcos is either cute or grotesque depending on your mood and aesthetic sensibilities. Personally, I think it takes ugly into a whole new dimension: I like it a lot. But then I'm possibly a bit mad.

→ The rear end with its stumpy Kamm tail was shaped purely for speed, but offers lots of interior space and interesting lines. A car with a Minivan wheelbase is crowded for four, but with just two it feels like a cathedral.

En route to shoot Mad Frank's Belgian Beast in Zeebrugge, I gave a Mini Marcos a proper European road test, during 2,300 miles and three weeks. Marcos Heritage is still very much in business and can still provide almost any body parts for any Marcos from 1963 to 2002, including bodyshells for all models and a complete Mini Marcos kit.

The Mini Marcos is a racing kit car developed in the early 1960s, based on the entire mechanicals of a Mini. The Mini in standard form wiped the floor with many racing and rally cars in the early 1960s mainly because of its incredible handling, and Minis stormed the Monte Carlo Rally with a 1-2-3 win: the French cheated but we all know who won.

A Mini Marcos did extremely well at Le Mans in 1966, coming 15th overall and being the only British entry to finish. It was technically a French entry in order to avoid being disqualified for being the wrong colour or whatever. It also achieved a flat-out speed of 140mph+ along the Mulsanne straight – impressive, as the engine was an off-the-shelf 1,275cc Mini Cooper S, fresh from the BMC competition department.

The Mini Marcos was and is so successful because it improves significantly on the abilities of the already remarkably competent Mini. It's lighter, its fibreglass monocoque is stronger and stiffer, its glasshouse is smaller and much lower, its centre of gravity is way down, and its longer Traveller/Van wheelbase aids stability.

The shape is either cute or horrible depending on your personal opinion, but it does the job: it's aerodynamically

very slippery and stable in aerodynamic terms, and the high rear roof and chopped-off Kamm tail work well at high speeds.

The Mini Marcos is still as good a proposition in 2009 as it was in 1965, and it's still the same car, apart from a hatchback and more interior space.

The Mini as a donor is far from outdated, and is even making a resurgence. Mini bits are more available now than they were a decade ago and remain cheap, at hobby prices rather than main-dealer prices. More new replica parts and performance goodies appear all the time.

Minis are also rusting as enthusiastically as ever, and from around 1990 the strapped-for-cash Rover company made them out of thinner metal but still failed to provide adequate rustproofing, so rotten later-model donor Minis with excellent mechanicals abound.

The Mini club scene, and for that matter the Mini

↑ The high bonnet line is caused by the Mini engine sitting on top of its integral gearbox. The view from the cockpit looks like that of a much larger and more expensive car.

26

Marcos club scene, are another excellent reason for getting involved with Minis – Mini people are enthusiastic, sociable, intelligent, helpful and just slightly crazy in the right sort of way.

So how did the three-week road test go? On the first day things did not look good. Britain's roads are in poor shape, and the seat in the Marcos had no lumbar support. The suspension is also brutally stiff, partly because the shell is lighter and stiffer than a Mini and partly because of hard low-profile tyres. The Mini suspension components, like the rest of the Mini parts, are standard and are just transferred from the old to the new shell. This car was deliberately built from a second-hand 60,000-mile 1991 Cooper without any improvements or refurbishment at all.

I finished the first day with a sore back, tired, and damp, as it was raining heavily. The car doesn't leak much, but it does steam up during monsoon weather. However, on day two I bought an inflatable neck pillow to use as a back support, and felt much better. Marcos seats can be ordered with lumbar support, so that's definitely worth doing. I also got used to the suspension, and when the sun came out and I found a big roundabout with nobody on it, the fun started.

When it comes to corners, the Mini Marcos is hilarious. None of this boring slowing-down business, you just pile in at full speed, turn the wheel and keep your foot down. I think that on the twisties a Mini Marcos would be very hard to beat with anything but a fairly serious competition car. It just goes round bends completely flat, no leaning, no squealing, just goes wherever you point it, at whatever ridiculous speed you choose. The only risk is that although a Marcos driver can charge into a roundabout at 60mph, everybody else has to crawl round at 25mph, so you have to go around them, and bear in mind that few of them are capable of paying attention or signalling.

Given some empty country roads, as instructed by Marcos Heritage boss Rory, I gave the Mini Marcos some revs and have seldom had so much fun from a cheap car. Being right down on the deck like a go-kart, with the fruity exhaust roaring away and the hedgerows hurtling past my ear in a green blur, it feels even faster than it is. A BMW type, upset at being overtaken, tried to intimidate me by tailgating, but chickened out after two corners: he didn't have a hope of keeping up, even with 200bhp to my 60.

There's something of a Tardis about the Mini Marcos – it looks tiny from the outside, but once you get inside there's an astonishing amount of room. A six-foot passenger with the seat right back couldn't touch the front firewall with his feet, it was so far away. I was

↑ LED rear lights add sparkle and update the decor, but that Kamm tail is timeless anyway: it doesn't look any better or worse than it did in 1966, unlike more fashion-driven designs.

→ Interior space in the Mini Marcos really is remarkable considering the size of the car, and the very low driving position is almost too comfy. Fortunately the stiff suspension will keep you awake.

travelling with a couple of wheely suitcases and there was plenty of room in the back for them, and when I took a friend with me to Belgium there was plenty of room for his kit as well.

The noise levels inside this particular car were quite high, but with plenty of padding under the carpet it wasn't interior noise so much as the roar from the air filter at the front and the sportsy exhaust tailpipe at the back. The car is a demonstrator, built to provide thrills and fun over a short blast on local country roads, not for touring Europe. Even so, I'd happily use it again on the same trip, although I would definitely soften the suspension if I was going to build one. Even if you compromised the razor-sharp handling a little with downrated suspension, a Mini Marcos would still handle better than pretty well everything else on the road.

Only having four gears might have been an issue, but in the event it was fine: the UK admits to having 63 million people jammed into a pretty small island, to which you can add an unknown but sizeable number of illegals, so the roads are crowded and slow even with petrol tax at piracy levels. The later Marcos shell allows the use of 13in wheels rather than the earlier 10in Mini wheels, so the gear ratios were just fine. Cruising at 70mph the engine was working but not howling, and the

1275 Cooper's 60bhp has enough muscle to carry quite a high final-drive ratio.

There's very little air resistance due to the excellent aerodynamics, so you could cruise at higher speeds, no bother. I'd use higher-profile tyres on 12in rims for a better ride, though.

The same aerodynamic properties that allowed a 140mph+ top speed at Le Mans can also give you astonishing fuel economy. The Cooper engine in the Marcos I was using gave pretty good fuel efficiency

↑ The transverse 60bhp Mini Cooper engine and transaxle has more room in the Mini Marcos engine bay than it does in a Mini, and the radiator goes in front rather than at the side. If your life is not scary enough, a 225bhp Honda engine can be used instead...

considering I was either giving it some exercise or stuck in a traffic jam, but if you used the smaller and cheaper 1,000cc A-series engine, with the right carburation and with the crank well balanced to allow you to use the revs when you wanted to charge about a bit, you could still enjoy pretty good performance… but you could be looking at 50mpg. Fuel mileage for fun weekend kit cars may not be an issue now, but, looking a few years ahead, a practical two-seater that sips petrol could be a very useful vehicle indeed as 'green' anti-car taxes go through the roof along with oil company profits.

The cost of a new Mini Marcos kit is currently around five grand, but all you then need is a complete scrap Mini and you're in business – the kit is comprehensive and there are no further costs. You can also knock off a couple of grand for a paint job, as the kits are supplied in coloured gelcoat. The car pictured is gelcoat-finished, and still gleams after three hard years of life as a demonstrator.

If you have doubts about the performance and reliability limitations, and the attention demands of ancient British engines and Lucas electricals driven hard and daily, that would not be unreasonable. What you need to know in that case is that lots of people are currently removing Mini engines and integral four-speed gearboxes, and are replacing them with 225bhp Honda Type R engines and five-speed boxes. The resultant performance is terrifying, partly because the power increase from the variable-profile Vtec cam comes in with a huge bang, and partly because the Type R diff is a brutal affair that needs the bulk of a heavy Honda shell to tame it. The cures are to use an ECU modification that brings the cam change in earlier, and to use a standard Honda LSD rather than the type R.

Nobody's done it yet, but if you can get a B-series Honda engine into a Mini you can get it in a Mini Marcos too. *Woo-hoo.* Top speed unknown, storming acceleration, and more or less the same astonishing handling. If I didn't already have too many projects…

Check out the Marcos Heritage website at www.rory.uk.com.

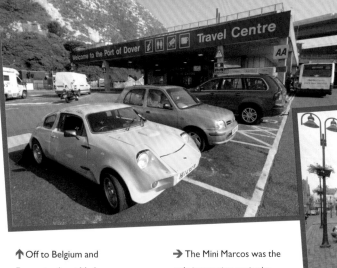

↑ Off to Belgium and France to shoot Mad Frank's V8 Mini in Zeebrugge. Looming over P&O's ferry terminal are the Green Cliffs of Dover.

→ The Mini Marcos was the only interesting car in the entire town of Diksmuide, Belgium: the crushing hand of the TUV and EU have banned everything but dullmobiles.

Tech

**Performance
and reliability !**

*Performance
et endurance !*

Les vingt-quatre heures
du Mans

MARCOS CARS COMPONENTS LIMITED
Greenland Mills,
Bradford-on-Avon,
Wiltshire, England
Telephone: Bradford-on-Avon 2971, 2972

↑ For Marcos in 1966, selling
cars paid for going racing, but
racing also helped sell cars.
(Courtesy of Billy Dulles)

ENGINE – Standard 1991 Mini Cooper S 1275, front-mounted radiator.

TRANSMISSION – Standard Cooper 1275 S four-speed with quickshift.

SUSPENSION – Standard rubber cones, uprated by shell weight reduction.

BRAKES – Standard Cooper S powered discs.

WHEELS AND TYRES – 6J x 13in Minilite alloys, with 175/50 x 13 Yokohamas.

INTERIOR – Marcos trim kit, seats, walnut dash, Moto-Lita steering wheel; donor Mini provides instruments, controls, steering column, pedals, door furniture and window winders.

EXTERIOR – Full GRP Marcos monocoque shell with glazing and some lights. Donor Mini provides mechanical and electrical components, subframes, brakes, suspension, steering, exhaust, door handles, lights etc.

The Psycho Twini

At first glance, Mike's Mini looks like a harmless Clubman.

TJC 654T

'WOOOOOOOO! WAAAAAAH! NAAAAAAAH! SIDEWAYS AAAARGH! WOOOOOOO! GO ON, BOOT IT! YEE-HAAAAA!' That was my Writer's Opinion box for Mike Smith's twin-Vauxhall-engined Clubman estate when I wrote about it in *MiniWorld* magazine: you won't have read it, though, because the Opinion box became a casualty of a redesign.

Mike's Clubman suffered the same fate. It was previously a harmless shopping trolley, minding its own business and crumbling gently into old age when it was rudely Frankensteined back to life as an unruly monster.

Vauxhall-engined Minis are scarier than Icelandic bank accounts. Despite that, just one 180bhp Vauxhall engine in his Clubman wasn't fast enough for Mike, so he added a second one. I've been frightened/exhilarated by Vauxhallated Minis before, even when driving on the track with a cage and good harnesses: they're either skittering towards the kitty litter or taking off like greased squirrels whenever they get a proper grip. You need to be well strapped in.

To achieve grip despite big power, front-wheel drive and no weight isn't easy. Quite an effective approach is to get rid of the suspension. On smooth straights, no worries: on bumpy racetrack corners with a cavalier approach taken to the corner kerbs, this means some time is spent airborne until the tyres grip again. Mike's car actually does have some suspension, although he's already changed 375lb AVO springs for 500lb ones in the search for grip.

The tyre choice is sorted, though – Yoko 888R cut slicks provide excellent grip even in the wet, but at a price. It's not that they're stupid-expensive, it's just that Mike only gets about 4,000 miles out of a set. But that's mostly because he's a maniac.

This Clubman Estate has 360bhp and four-wheel drive, and Mike is still getting the hang of learning to drive it in a straight line, never mind turning corners.

The noise when both engines are started is incredible. The exhausts both come out the back, and oddly enough it's the longer front-engine exhaust pipe that's the noisier. Off we go for a spin on damp Birmingham rural roads, looking for a place to play. Having found somewhere without anything hard to hit if the car decides to take a side excursion into the scenery, Mike checks behind, revs both engines and dumps the clutches. The stereo roar is ear-shredding, and the kick in the back is exhilarating: this is dragstrip acceleration, not road-car power. When the ferocity of the acceleration lifts the front of the car more or less off the deck, Mike's home-made traction control reduces power to the front engine, to stop it grenading itself. As the passing greenery blurs, more of the wheels get a grip, and Mike snatches gearchanges while sawing wildly at the steering wheel to keep the car pointing forwards. The engines yammer dementedly, and the car squirms and wriggles as the diffs brutally and randomly direct power to assorted wheels, according to whim.

↑ The car has a bit of a stance and big wheels, but still looks like a nice little Clubby rather than a scary psycho beast. The rollcage peeping through the rear windows suggests that all is not as it seems.

← Even the twin exhausts look like minor showing-off, but there's one for each engine. One Vauxhall engine in a Mini is scary enough, without another one at the other end.

↙ The second engine peeps coyly between the seats.

The Clubman's best quarter-mile time is 12.69 seconds at 117mph, and the best 0–60mph time so far is 3.9 seconds. Top speed is governed to 155mph. Fuel efficiency is excellent with cruising economy of up to 50mpg, but that's with the back engine switched off.

Birmingham is the birthplace of Balti cuisine, which may have provided Mike with the original subconscious inspiration for the car – Balti chili Jalfrezi is hot and tasty stuff, and like this Mini it makes you sweat and helps you to develop strong sphincter muscles.

The Clubman replaced Mike's previous car, a Nissan Skyline. He developed the Skyline to 550bhp, but they're heavy beasts at 1,600kg and need 1,000bhp to be properly lively. His Skyline's 3.5 seconds to 60mph wasn't bad, but getting much more out of it would have become disproportionately expensive. Getting 1,000bhp reliably out of one Skyline engine is very expensive indeed: it pushes many other components past breaking point and ultimately produces less speed than using an 850kg car and building two 355bhp engines.

Mike likes Vauxhall engines: 200 fairly bombproof normally-aspirated bhp is comparatively cheap and easy with forged pistons and steel H-beam rods, and Vauxhall spares are reasonably priced.

The Vauxhall gearboxes and final-drive ratios were designed for 13in wheels rather than 10in, but even with 60% profile tyres there's enough torque to get away pretty sharpish, and of course if you can save one gearchange on the dragstrip with tall gearing, that's worth a big chunk of a precious second.

Conveniently, the Clubman shell was already halfway converted to take a Vauxhall engine, with an AMT engine frame fitted. AMT no longer make engine frames, but www.16Vminiclub.co.uk has alternative sources if the idea of a Vauxhall or dual-Vauxhall Mini blows your frock up.

The front engine arrangements were therefore fairly straightforward, although extra tasks such as shifting the alternator to the other side of the engine added much time to the build. A more demanding matter was designing and fabricating the arrangements for fitting the second engine. It's a similar arrangement to the front engine/gearbox/suspension setup and also uses an AMT frame, except that instead of a steering rack, the redundant rear steering arms are connected to the chassis and used to adjust the rear tracking rather than to steer the car. It was also a challenge figuring out what to attach the frame to, as an estate Mini with no rear subframe is basically an empty tin box. Most of the rear floor went, along with half of each rear suspension turret. The rollcage helped by providing places to weld to, and a subframe was also made and welded to the floorpan.

The main challenges came with the electronics and the gear linkages. Mike used a DTA E48EXP ECU on a custom loom with custom traction control, which he made himself for a budget of 50 quid. If one engine speeds up dramatically compared to the other, its power is automatically reduced. The traction system also lights up LEDs on the dash, which is functional as well as cool. The main instrument is a Digidash data logger/speedo that can be switched to display and record the activities of either engine. Other instruments are simply duplicated, including the big analogue tachos.

The gear linkages on the front engine were straightforward, and the clutch pedal simply works twin master cylinders like a normal street/competition-biased brake system, with a servo on the rear clutch. The rear engine's gear lever, if left unaltered, would be a foot or so outside the back doors, so both planes of gear lever movement had to be replaced with a cable arrangement going to the single central gear lever in the cabin. That was hard going, but it now works pretty well. More bracketing had to be made to get rid of flex in the cable system, and much of the rear gearchange trouble was finally cured by replacing the front engine mounts with harder ones: it was movement of the engine (and thus the gearbox and gear lever) that was fouling up the linkage to the rear gearbox. There's a pin that disconnects the cable and leaves the rear engine in neutral when it's switched off.

↑Fitting the rear engine took serious inventive abilities: the Clubman Estate monocoque wasn't designed for either two engines or 360bhp.

↓Two injected ECU-controlled engines meant miles of multi-coloured electrical spaghetti.

↑Substantial conrods with ARP bolts reduce the likelihood of a rod doing an Alien through the crankcase, even with nitrous and cheeky throttle action.

Many problems [these are called *Issues* if you're from California] arose during the build, but they were all sorted. The handbrake required thought, because there wasn't one. Using four front hubs means no handbrake or mounts exist, so a mechanical caliper system and cables had to be designed, sourced and fitted. The double clutch was a bear to use until Mike fitted a servo to the rear clutch: now it's fine. The cylinder head on the front engine went porous after a few thousand miles and had to be replaced, which was just boring and annoying. Fortunately Mike keeps a spare engine in the back. Likewise when a throttle trumpet nut came loose and fell into the engine, wrecking a head and piston, it was a

← Starting the engines involves flashy switchgear and drama, and why not? Just using two ignition keys would be dull. Black box is the LED display for traction control.

↖ Fuse and relay board would frighten an IBM engineer. On the other hand, Joseph Lucas wasn't involved in any of it.

↖ Sorting out the gear change was tricky: the gear lever operates the front box conventionally and the rear one via a cable system.

↓ Even without nitrous, the acceleration of a 360bhp, 4WD Mini is breathtaking.

ENGINES – Two Vauxhall C20XE 16V 1,998cc units, uprated oil pumps, Eagle H-girder pattern steel rods with ARP rod bolts, Mahle pistons with 2mm valve cutouts for future high-lift cams. ECU, DTA E48EXP in custom loom, wideband closed loop Lambda systems, home-designed traction control. Vauxhall beige injectors, QED DTH throttle bodies, ITG foam air filters. Custom 2.25in stainless exhaust systems. Front engine radiator, South African spec Cavalier Turbo. Rear engine radiator, Cavalier GSi. Two Jaguar XKR fuel pumps. About 180bhp at each flywheel, 355bhp each with nitrous.

TRANSMISSION – F20 Vauxhall clutches and gearboxes with standard ratios. Rear gear selector forks reversed, custom cable system replaces rear gearbox shaft-based gearchange. Front diff, Quaife ATB LSD with 3.42:1 final drive, rear diff standard Vauxhall 3.55:1. Driveshafts 4 x AMT custom one-piece, with Vauxhall inner CVs and Austin Allegro outer CVs.

BRAKES – No servo, Goodridge braided hoses. Custom pedal box with front/rear bias adjuster bar. Metro Turbo four-pot calipers all round, vented discs. Custom handbrake calipers and cable.

SUSPENSION – Coilover adjustable AVO shocks all round, with 500lb springs. Rose-jointed adjustable arms top and bottom. Mini steering rack.

WHEELS AND TYRES – White Weller steels 5.5J x 13, with Toyo 888R 185/60 x 13.

INTERIOR – Sparco buckets, harnesses, FIA-spec rollcage, two AMT engine frames. ATB Digidash II connected to both engines. RPM x 2, oil temp x 2, water temp x 2, oil pressure x 2. Custom relay and fuse panel.

EXTERIOR – Gp5 arches, steel flip front. Round nose front signals.

good job he had a spare engine in the front to drive home on.

Mike's now fitting a nitrous setup from the Wizards of Nos, with a 150bhp shot at the front and a 200bhp shot at the rear, adding 350bhp at the crankshafts. The engines are built to handle this, but the gearboxes may not take a joke that funny. If you want to keep up to date with Mike's progress, check in with www.twinenginemini.co.uk now and again and see what happened next. The dashboard is due to be flocked soon, and there is talk of carpets.

Mini Kit Cars

←↑ Domino Cars saved many a moribund Mini from death by oxidisation: simply dismantle the Mini, move all the bits a few feet over, bolt them into the Pimlico or Premier's immortal GRP tub, fold the roof down and enjoy.

↑ The Mini's power package has always been an extremely convenient source of power for kit-car use: cheap, plentiful, neat, small, and comes on its own subframe.

Minis have always provided an excellent package for kit car designers and enthusiasts. The whole powertrain, steering and front suspension assembly comes out in one go, and is even mounted on a convenient subframe, on to which you can bolt your own ideas. Several of the top mad Minis in this book are or were available in kit form.

Some, such as the Domino family, simply repackaged the whole Mini mechanical set and wiring into a new shell that was more amusing than the original Mini, and 100% more rust-resistant. Minis were never properly protected against rust, which is one more reason why they appealed, and still appeal, to kit car builders: many an otherwise perfectly good Mini has crumbled beyond hope of even a pub-bought MOT and has been rescued and recycled into a kit car. The price of a seriously crumbled Mini, up until very recently, has been in the low two figures. Even now there are MOT-failed basket-cases available for the asking.

A Domino Pimlico/Premier is basically an improved Mini. It's convertible, lighter, stronger, stiffer and cheaper than a nice standard Mini, but it's still recognisably and spiritually a Mini. It has deep, strong sills, wheel arches designed for 12in or 13in wheels and no body seams, as they're irrelevant on GRP cars. Dominos have been in production off and on since 1986, and only just finally died in 2008 – the last owners of the company couldn't even make the project break even, due mainly to current levels of UK commercial premises rates, Health and Safety expenses, and liability risks.

Most designers using the Mini abandoned the original Issigonis body shape and went off in their own direction. The GTM uses quite a lot of the Mini donor, including the engine/powertrain package, but it's relocated to the back of the car to create a rear-Mini-engined two-seater sports car with excellent handling and grip. The steering arms are simply connected to brackets on the chassis and become adjustable track-control arms, and quite often cars like the GTM use a second front subframe in the front of the car to provide steering and suspension. The GTM pictured here will also be reviewed in the Fresh Ayre section of *Kit Car* magazine.

The Mini Marcos is another example of the best features of the Mini design being hijacked and re-shelled into something faster and more amusing, with even better handling than the Mini. The GTM might have the edge over a Marcos on the track, being mid-engined – it would be fun to find out. The GTM certainly has the edge over the Marcos as far as looks go, but unlike the Marcos, the Mini-based GTMs are no longer in production, having evolved into a Rover Metro-based descendant.

Getting well away from the Mini shape was the Hustler, from late car designer William Towns. He used Mini donor packages for several city car projects, but the Hustler took off and became a relatively good seller in kit car terms, with 500 sold. The Hustler owners' club used to visit William annually for a picnic until he died. I spent a day with him once for a magazine interview, and found him a thoroughly nice man. He advised me that when designing cars one should never use a straight line. I must have looked rather taken aback at that, given that he had designed the notably curve-deficient Hustler and the equally angular Aston Martin Lagonda, but he went on to explain that you can use lines that *look* straight, but they must never actually *be* straight. I've always found his Lagonda aesthetically indigestible, like most people, but his DBS is a top piece of automotive art.

The Mini-based Hustler originally only had four wheels, but could also be bought with six wheels: you simply added a second rear Mini subframe behind the first one. Although the concept evolved to become bigger and finished up with Maxi power, the theme of a mobile greenhouse with huge sliding glass doors was retained. The Hustler is basically a cross between a conservatory and a Mini Moke. I haven't driven a Hustler, but I imagine it must feel a bit like riding a Vespa scooter, apart from being warm, comfy, relatively safe and not requiring a claustrophobic crash helmet and shoes with drain holes. The Hustler's original GRP and steel bodywork was later replaced by plywood, which if cleverly used as in Hustlers and early Marcos GTs is very light and extremely strong.

28

← William Towns's Hustler started off as a straightforward GRP and steel rebodying design exercise for a Mini. The enormous glass area would have cooked occupants, but the vast doors can be slid back to turn it into a mobile gazebo.

→ The GTM started off as a mid-engined Mini, and continued to evolve: it's now become the GTM Libra, and uses the Rover/MG K-series engine. It's still a stiff and strong GRP monocoque.

↓ This example of the Hustler has evolved to six wheels, plywood construction and a Maxi engine to pull the increased weight.

The Beauford still has some traces of Mini DNA, but diluted almost to herbalist percentages. If you looked at a new Beauford kit you'd just see something faintly and familiarly Mini-ish. The original rather clever idea of the Beauford was to create a huge 1930s-style limousine for a small budget. A large chunk of capital-hungry development time was saved by nicking bits of other cars and putting them together.

The chassis under the first Beaufords was a very simple but strong ladderframe. The front end of the bodywork, the grille and long bonnet, are inspired by Packard. The whole back end of the car was a Mini shell plonked on top of the chassis. The rolling gear was provided by a Cortina. Job done, basically.

The result was a vast engine bay that would take any engine you cared to fit. A common choice was the Datsun straight six – reliable, smooth and cheap. Most Beaufords are wedding limos: they do the job for peanuts compared to the usual baggy old 1970s Rolls-Royce Silver Shadow with its potentially breathtaking repair bills.

In kit car design, door-hinges, door shuts, window winders and so on are an expensive nightmare, possibly the most complex area to design, so for Beauford to use the Mini shell saved a bundle and worked really well. As time went on the Mini/Beauford shell was remade in GRP, lost its roof, was extended, and had its curved windscreen replaced by two flat screens in basically the same frame. The doors on their two-door models remain modified steel Mini doors, applying the sound design principle that if it ain't broke, don't fix it. The glass is different and quarter-lights have been added, but the doors are still Mini. I have road-tested a Beauford, and it

was thoroughly nice: smooth, comfy, solid, and silent apart from a baritone rumble from the exhaust.

There is something of a divide in the Mini world between those who revere proper Minis and those who throw the rulebook out of the window, but as far as most Mini people are concerned you can enjoy both. I write for *MiniWorld*, which loves mad Minis as long as they retain the Mini shape. So you'll find stories about Z-Cars with GRP shells, which are kits rather than Minis, but you'll only rarely find a mention of Marcos or GTM.

I also write for *Kit Car* magazine, which is a different world: modern kit cars are regarded as a bit pussy if they can't do at least 150mph, get to 60mph in three seconds and crash survivably into the Armco at 130mph. *Top Gear* avoids mentioning kit cars because they make production sports cars look girly: Clarkson and *Top Gear* stay safely in the unimaginative Ferrari/Porsche-worshipping mainstream. If you've read this far you're already outside that boring box. In addition to the 200mph Ultima kits charging around there are still hundreds of old Mini kit cars bimbling about – once you eliminate rust, Minis can live forever. Looking at the fun-per-quid ratio, it's hard to beat a Mini-based kit car.

Paul Banham is a notable kit car designer who has used Minis and Metros as donors. He's not exactly mad, but he does insist on doing things his own way: if other people think he's mad he doesn't really care. He could

make serious money if he applied his talents to something commercial, but he keeps coming back to inventing new kit cars, even after blowing himself up in a workshop explosion recently. He can't smell any more after years of breathing fibreglass fumes, and a chemical gas leak made itself known via a huge explosion when he switched on his workshop lights. Fortunately he was still only halfway through the doorway and got blown out rather than up. Although quite significantly sautéed at the time, he's basically okay now and still designing and making kit cars.

⬇ The installation of the Mini engine/box/ suspension in the GTM is still as it comes out of the Mini – it's just moved to the mid-rear position for rear-wheel drive and better handling and balance.

He doesn't like mechanicals or electricals, so he usually leaves all that intact, cuts a donor production car down to its sills, adds a steel frame to brace it all and then puts something completely unexpected on top of the result. He's made a Porsche Spyder out of a Skoda, he's made something that resembles an Audi TT out of a Metro, and his most recent project is an XK180 replica made out of a chopped-down XJS. This was quite easy,

as the XKR and the XK180 were built by Jaguar the same way: they cut the panels off an XJS monocoque, attached some new ones and presented it as the shiny new XKR. The main difference between the two is that Paul's entire kit costs about the same as a replacement engine for an XKR.

Paul's most unexpected Mini kit was his Sprint, which looks almost exactly like a Frogeye Sprite. He was unable to resist improving it by adding a bootlid, which is how you can tell the difference between the Frogeye and the Banham. The car uses a Mini floorpan, subframes and mechanicals, cut right down and then stiffened with a steel frame, on to which replica Frogeye panels are mounted. The Mini engine is even correct for a Sprite, but is fitted the wrong way round and on top of the gearbox. I tested one of these, and thought it was fab: it felt and sounded quite like the Sprite I used to own way back. The Mini rack and pedals are still used, but the angles of them are greatly improved over the Mini, as you sit well back from the engine package. Banham's kits generally require a lot of welding and bodywork effort, but are also inexpensive, so abandoned projects abound. If you want one, check out www.autos.groups.yahoo.com/groups/sprintists, which is a club for Banham Sprint owners and builders.

If kit Minis in general appeal to you, my *Kit Car Manual* is also published by Haynes, and it gives you a good general picture of the kit-car world and mentions

← The Beauford is a rather magnificent 1930s-style limo with a Mini-based bodyshell at the back. Many of them have a Saturday job as a wedding car. *(Courtesy of Steve Hole, totalkitcar.com)*

→ The Banham Sprint uses Mini mechanicals for a weirdly authentic replica. *(Courtesy of Madabout-Kitcars.com)*

Mini kits quite frequently. If my smartarse blathering after 28 chapters is becoming too annoying to cope with, ignore the last suggestion and amble off to a kit car show (dates can be found on www.kit-cars.com or www.totalkitcar.com) and visit the club areas, where there will be many Mini-based kit cars to examine, and enthusiasts delighted to tell you all about them. My website www.ayrspeed.com also has lots of kit-car action on it.

→ The Sprint's engine is the correct A-series for the Sprite, but is used the wrong way round. *(Courtesy of Madabout-Kitcars.com)*

→ My own Swallow trike design used the complete Mini package from a scrap car, with a single Mini rear trailing arm at the back. That solved many design problems in one go, and with its long wheelbase it handled very well.

← If you don't believe me about the Beauford's Mini rear bodywork, just check out the inside of that door. Is that from a Mini or what? *(Courtesy of Steve Hole, totalkitcar.com)*

Mini Mouse

It's a Mini Van, Jim, but not as we know it. Only the grille remains standard on this van – almost everything else has been rodded. Welded-in bumpers and frenched lights are the primary frontal features.

Paul Saulnier's Mini Van is a serious street rod, in the Boyd Coddington or Chip Foose arena. Paul is a member of both Mini clubs and street rod clubs, so it looks as though he decided to save time and blow all their minds with a car that was both at the same time. Street rods are quite often mid-life-crisis cars ordered by rich men who pay others to design and make their rods for them, so the budgets can be in the hundreds of thousands of dollars, but Mini Mouse was conceived and built with imagination and creativity rather than a bottomless chequebook.

The invoices are nonetheless impressive. The shell only cost a grand but the engine and drivetrain cost $15,000, the bodywork and paint $18,000 and the exhaust system $3,000. The total of around 40 grand is low-budget for a rod, but an impressive commitment for a Mini.

Paul is a gearhead from way back. His first car was a 1928 Oldsmobile, with 16,000 miles on the clock, bought illegally without his parents' knowledge and garaged in the next town. He would borrow licence plates from friends and drive it around at nights and weekends. British cars are in his blood as well – he still owns a 1959 Austin-Healey rebuilt from wreckage, so Lucas electrics and enthusiastic body rusting don't worry him.

Drag racing is also in his blood, and he used to run a 1927 Ford at the strip until the third blown engine, after which he got bored with rebuilding the engine and sold the car. That drag-racing experience with its expensive bangs is the reason for the extremely strong bottom end of the Chevy V8 in Mini Mouse. This motor has definitely been built not to blow up. The other hangover from

dragstrip days is the memory of the rush that the Ford gave him when it got to the other end of the strip in one piece in 9.2 seconds.

The Mini Van showed up in 2003 as a bare shell, spotted by his son Phil on eBay. After the usual finger-crossing tension theirs was the top bid, and the van was soon heading for Massachusetts. Phil's 00101111110101010 skills on the computer also came in very useful during the hunting of parts, both Mini and custom.

Paul is a civil engineer and usually deals with very big things. Minis, particularly in America, are almost comically small things. Putting a big thing in a very small thing appealed to him, and the fact that Chevrolet's original 1950s 265CI (4,300cc) V8 was known as the Mouse Motor allowed him to christen his car Mini Mouse without sounding embarrassingly cute.

A Chevy V8 will visibly fit in the back of a Mini Van, but in order to see exactly how it would fit and how it would have to be mounted, Paul made a full-sized styrofoam replica engine. He could then get inside the van beside the foam engine and move the mock-up around to figure out the drivetrain and suspension frame design. With the frame conceptualised and measurements taken, the bottom of the van was cut out and the bodywork bracing structures and suspension mounts were welded in. The structure ended up resembling the suspension turrets of the Pontiac from which the rear suspension was taken. The finished rollcage/chassis is mounted to the van's shell and supports the engine and gearbox as well as the Pontiac

↑ You still wouldn't think there was a monster V8 in the back rather than just a picnic basket and a couple of show prizes.

29

→ From the rear three-quarters view, the stance of the Mini is easy to appreciate: a lot of thought went into the wheel/arch/ride height equation.

↓ Frisky Chevy 350 with Porsche G50 gearbox and transaxle is a killer combo that fits the Mini Van very neatly indeed. Suspension turrets were designed and built to suit the tried-and-tested Pontiac Fiero rear suspension assembly.

suspension struts. The engine still has to be removable, as the alternative would be to send in Chevrolet-trained chimpanzee mechanics. Properly trained chimp mechanics are quite rare, although some professional mechanical work I've seen suggests that untrained monkey mechanics are everywhere.

The engine is a monster, although the amount of bang per buck is actually relatively modest. 427bhp out of 5.7 litres is not extreme, but that bottom end with Keith Black pistons, forged rods, ARP bolts and a toughened crank would probably handle twice the current power output. Paul would like more power later, and he has the options of supercharging, turbocharging or nitrous oxide to liven things up. The engine is also classic American muscle with some purist subtleties about it: 'pink' rods are genuine GM factory performance rods, still available but originally fitted

to GM performance engines in the 1960s. These rods had a splash of pink paint to identify them in the factory. So 'pink rods' for a Chevy enthusiast mean special authentic factory goodies, in the same way that 'S brakes' mean something to a Mini bunny but not to most people.

Ceramic-coated Sanderson block-hugger headers will again not mean much to Mini people, but they're free-flow exhaust manifolds that hug the block as closely as possible while still achieving reasonably well-matched primary pipe lengths. The coating keeps the heat in, which helps keep the gasflow fast and the engine bay temperatures lower. The Edelbrock 650CFM carb with mechanical secondaries is a four-choke monster, the second two chokes of which are controlled mechanically rather than by vacuum, so you can feel the change on the throttle pedal. By way of comparison, a 1½in SU flows about 140cu ft per minute as against the Edelbrock's 650CFM. The top end of the engine is pretty high-spec with serious cams and gasflow, allowing plenty of options for more power later. Currently, Mini Mouse is expected to comfortably crack the ten-second barrier on the quarter-mile as Paul's old Ford used to do, which means a 0–60mph time in the three-second area.

The gearbox is a G50 Porsche five-speed gearbox/transaxle from a 911, with suspension and driveshafts provided by a Pontiac Fiero, an underrated mid-rear-engined 1980s sports car. The G50 is a good choice, stronger than the previous Porsche transmission. It's used upside down and the linkage comes out of the side rather than the back, as the original linkages would have finished up poking out through the back doors. The box is also reversed, as the van is mid-rear-engined and the Porsche is rear-engined,

with the weight all behind the axle like a Beetle. Hence its reputation for dodgy handling.

Turning the box upside down and the wrong way round: easy to write, somewhat harder to achieve. The Fiero shafts, struts and hubs have been proven strong enough to handle V8 power, as many people have stuffed big V8s into Fieros with great success. Mini Mouse's half-shafts are hybrid Porsche/Pontiac and quite short. The rear wheels and tyres had to be wide enough to provide grip for 400lb/ft+ of torque, but they also had to fit under the body in the right way stylistically. A tyre-smoke show doesn't do it for Paul, he wants action.

At the front, the cooling system and fuel cell occupy the engine bay. The fuel cell is shaped to allow air to flow smoothly through the radiator and past the tank to the wheel well vents. The Audi radiator is quite small but deep, and its position, its big twin fans and the long coolant lines to the engine make it very efficient.

With the structure sorted, the next task was to get the bodywork up to the same standard as the engine bay. There's major steelwork in this van. Dual chassis frame rails in 2in x 4in steel run along both sides of the car under the bodywork, and connect the rollcage to the front wheel arches. The exterior door hinges were removed and replaced by new rear-mounted hinges, so the remotely controlled doors now open from the front, suicide style. The subtly altered bonnet also pops open remotely and opens the 'wrong' way. The body panel changes are all steel, and the body kit is a one-off. Neat touches include a single screen-top wiper, power windows and the welded-in front bumper. Every seam in the body

was opened up, butt-welded and smoothed over, and the gutters were removed, restyled and replaced. Ron Melanson was the major bodywork dude involved.

The interior had to match the exterior, so it was completely created from scratch. The main feature of the vertical central console is the Art Deco-styled Vintage Air control panel. (Yes, of course it's air-conditioned – what did you expect?) The rest of that central console is minimalist, finished in engine-turned aluminium, and sports just a few lights and the ignition switch: less is more. Dakota Digital provided the futuristic and again minimalist instrumentation – all you see is a dark panel unless something's happening, but the range of information the dash provides is extensive once the engine is started. Very cool indeed. The electrics are custom, starting with a 20-circuit fuse box with ten relays and working outwards from there. Clayton Tomasetti's wiring expertise came in useful here. Steering is by a generic Flaming River rod-style tilt column, a potentially useful idea for UK Mini builders. Apart from anything else, it would be nice to get rid of the bus-like steering wheel angle that comes with a Mini rack and column, and that's instantly achieved by fitting a tilt steering column.

The seats are modified and retrimmed Fiero, and the driver's harness is a five-point drag-legal item so the car will be ready to rock when Paul is. The door action is in tune with the rest of the car. Remote electric suicide doors. Cool. What takes the doors just a little further is the detail. The Mini's original inner door handles are at the top of the door: not good enough. Paul had to rework the whole system to shift them to the bottom so that the

↑ Frenched tripod rod lights and chrome trims bring big bling: they don't light the road up very accurately, but who cares...

↖ The specially shaped fuel cell under the bonnet provides clear cooling fan airflow.

← Suicide doors are cool and unexpected on a Mini. The bonnet opens the wrong way as well.

↓ A blue and silver theme runs through the whole car. The interior is comfy as well as visually very stylish. The Dakota Digital dashboard fits in very well with the dramatic styling.

↑ The central vertical console is a very cool piece of styling, topped by an Art Deco air conditioning control panel.

→ The rear wheels are still reasonably in proportion to the front ones, so it still looks like a Mini rather than a psycho killer beast. The correct tyre contact patch for the weight gets the best grip.

door trim would look better. The door trimming itself is not just matching blue and silver vinyl, though – stitched into the material but without the distraction of a different colour is a trad flame job, a reference to old-school street rod styling. It's sort of compulsory for cars with a rod inclination, but it can be done with subtlety or without.

An interesting revelation is that with such a major project, Paul felt there was no light at the end of the tunnel until one day he actually found himself driving the car. That moment of triumph as Mini Mouse rumbled around the block for the first time was brief, though, as the car ran out of petrol within a couple of hundred yards.

Many, many projects fall foul of the seemingly endless and daunting list of Stuff To Do: kit-car builders suggest a couple of ideas. The first is to ignore the frightening big picture and concentrate on one section at a time, for example the brakes. Second, do something every single day, even if it's just tidying up and cleaning tools. After 365 small somethings, big progress is made. Paul was lucky that his wife Nancy, although oblivious to the dynamics, aesthetics and hoot value of V8 Minis, was supportive in the cheerful Mini-wife way: 'I'm happy if you're happy.'

Paul says the most fun he has nowadays with Mini Mouse is standing back from the car, watching people's reactions and listening to their comments. But maybe the top fun is still to come: he hasn't been out on the dragstrip yet to check out the car's theoretically estimated 9.2-second, 140mph quarter-mile.

ENGINE – 350CI (5.7-litre) Chevrolet mouse motor (.030 over) with nodular prepared and indexed crank, GM 'pink' (shot-peened and Magnafluxed) forged steel rods with ARP Wavelock bolts, Keith Black hypereutectic 10.3:1 pistons, Childs & Albert ZZ Gapdura Moly file fit rings. Comp Cams Custom series (110 centreline, 488-490 lift corrected 1.6 = 520/522 lift, 226/228 duration). Cloyes true roller rockers, Comp Cams hi-output cam lifter set, Comp Cams XE chrome moly pushrods. Edelbrock Aluminium Performer Heads with revised combustion chambers, severe duty 2.02/1.60 valves. HEI distributor, Spiral Core 8mm plug leads, Edelbrock Performer 650CFM carburettor with mechanical secondary chokes on Edelbrock Performer polished aluminium dual plane intake manifold, Sanderson Block Hugger ceramic-coated exhaust manifolds, custom fabricated 304 stainless steel 2.5in exhaust system with Pacesetter 304 stainless quick-release flex joints and dual Edelbrock SDT 304 stainless steel mufflers, by Dave's Custom Creations, Charlton, Mass. Audi 5000 radiator, Vintage Air condenser, twin 12in electric fans (1400CFM each), vented wheel wells. Porsche side-mount water pump, Edelbrock electric fuel pump and filter. 427bhp, 418lb/ft at the crank. Expected performance 9.2-second quarter-mile at 140mph.

TRANSMISSION – Porsche G50 transaxle converted to run inverted/reversed and converted to side shift: 1st, 3.1538; 2nd, 1.7895; 3rd, 1.2692; 4th, 0.8572; 5th, 0.6774. G50/930 Kevlar high-performance clutch disc. Gearbox parts Renegade Hybrids, Las Vegas: setup, California Motor Sports. Clutch pedal raised 1.5in and lengthened 2.5in to increase throw and leverage. Custom high-strength half-shafts (Porsche/Fiero hybrids) 40% limited slip differential, 3.444 final drive.

BRAKES – Mini dual system, ³⁄₁₆in stainless lines, some braided hoses. Wilwood proportioning valve, Summit Racing line lock. Front, 8.4in Metro four-pot discs; rear, Pontiac Fiero competition 11in discs.

SUSPENSION – Front, Mini with Hi-Los. Back, Pontiac Fiero Competition coilover struts, bump-steer upgrade kit. Detachable wheelie bars for dragstrip.

WHEELS AND TYRES – Front, 5J x 13 Minilites with diamond-cut lip, P165/65R13 Bridgestone Potenza tyres. Rear, 6J x 15 Minilites with diamond-cut lip, P225/50R15 BF Goodrich G Force TA Drag Radials.

INTERIOR – Pontiac Fiero seats, cut down 6in and reupholstered. Driver's harness RCI five-point drag-racing SFI-rated, passenger harness four-point. Custom rollcage surrounds engine compartment. Scratch-built rear bulkhead with window, insulated for sound, with engine access panel. Flaming River tilt steering column, X-Force 330mm steering wheel, blue leather/silver wood. Renegade custom gear lever and box with X-Force blue and silver aluminium gear knob. Scratch-built all-steel dash and centre console covers. Vintage Air heating and air conditioning unit, carries A/C vents, miscellaneous switches and lights. Dakota Digital VFD3X-1002 instrumentation with Teal lighting: water temp, oil pressure, fuel level, dimmer adjustable, brake failure indicator, high-beams, direction indicators, tacho, speedo. Custom wiring including 'It's a Snap' 20-circuit panel, ten relays, power doors, windows, bonnet, and rear doors.

EXTERIOR – 2in x 4in frame rails from front wheel wells to rear suspension, front bumper welded to body. All-steel ground effect panels with air dam to improve cooling, all body seams cut, butt-welded and smoothed. Roof gutter removed and reshaped over the doors, bonnet corners rounded and hood hinged from the front with remote power opener. Wiper holes filled, one wiper relocated over windscreen. Exterior door hinges removed and doors converted to front opening. Sliding glass windows removed. Power windows and power door latches installed with remote operation. Custom steel sills/ground effect panels and wheel arches, side scoop to bring cool air into engine compartment, rolled rear valance with ventilated centre section. Rear doors modified to internal hinges, Chevy 'Suburban' style windows, licence plate cut-out, power opener. Frenched LED tail lights and third brake light. Frenched Tristar halogen headlights with centre blue dots. Other body lights are LED, including parking, brakes and indicators. DuPont Hot Hues three-stage pearl paint, Psycho Silver and Blue Mood.

Posh Minis

The Wolseley Hornet featured a markedly different front end, with its own bumpers, grillework, front panel and bonnet. Some posh BMC/BL rebadging treatments were grotesque, notably the Vanden Plas Allegro, but this all works rather well.

The Mini was and is one of the few classless cars. Unlike most, it carried no particular status or wealth connotations, and was no more or less of a status symbol than an iPod is today.

The Mini was a direct descendant of the 1920s Austin Seven, which was an even more radical mini-car that also had four seats but was even shorter and narrower than a Mini. Austin Sevens were also radically modified and raced, and that tradition continues in the Mini. In fact the Austin-badged version of the first Mini was called the Seven or Se7en.

As a universally clever, small, cheap, useful and stylish object, and as a design icon in its own right, the Mini has always been able to dance around in the minefield of the British social status system without a care.

However, some people felt that in standard form it did not adequately reflect their superior social or financial status, and some weren't bothered about looking posh but simply wanted something different with more comfort, more style, more chrome, more boot space and more widgets to play with.

BMC themselves provided upmarket versions of the Mini, which were the Riley Elf and the Wolseley Hornet. BMC and then British Leyland had been indulging in 'badge engineering' since the 1952 merger, having acquired many British brands including at various times Austin, Morris, Wolseley, Riley, Triumph, Jaguar, Land-Rover, Austin-Healey, Innocenti, Standard, and the coachbuilder Vanden Plas, as the company mutated through BMC, BMH, BLMC, BL, and Rover before the remnants were bought by Nanjing Automobile. BMW, sadly, owns the Triumph and Riley brand-name rights, so we can expect those respected marques to be exhumed

from their graves, spinning or not, and given the Rolls-und-Royce treatment when the BMW badge premium has completely evaporated.

An example of 1950s badge engineering was the mid-sized MG/Wolseley saloon, resembling a gentlemen's club in both pace and décor. The slow 1,500cc B-series-engined version of this hefty car was badged as an MG Magnette, and the painfully slow 1,250cc XPAG-engined version was badged as a Wolseley 4/44… although it was the one with the MG engine. I used to drive one, which is how I learned about the need for percussive maintenance on SU fuel pumps. These cars were upmarket from Austins, but downmarket from Rovers. There was also a similar but larger and faster car known as the Riley Pathfinder, fitted with what could be regarded as the last real Riley engine with twin cams, twin SUs, 2,443cc and 110bhp. My first experience of speeds over 100mph was in an uncle's Pathfinder. The uncle in question later lost the plot and bought an Austin Allegro and a beige cardigan.

The social status of cars is intriguing me at the

↑ This is one of the rare Heinz 57 Hornets, with its Crayford convertible roof folded down. The extra boot space and foot of bodywork are nice, but rather miss the point of a Mini.

↖ The Wolseley is posh but not as posh as the Riley, so it only has a small patch of walnut dashboard.

← The Radford dash is seriously posh. A slab of veneered wood is decorated with the full complement of gleaming chrome-bezelled clocks and an impressive array of switches.

The Wolseley pictured is one of 57 'Heinz' cars presented in 1966 as competition prizes after having been converted to open-tops by body specialists Crayford. The Heinz Wolseleys came with leather seats, insulated food cabinets, kettles and electric points, picnic hampers, radios and make-up trays. These were presumably for mascara repair after a brisk windy run to the British coast with the roof off for a picnic in a seafront car park, where 1960s Brits liked to sit shivering in the car, munching cheese sandwiches, drinking tepid tea from tartan vacuum flasks and watching grey waves thumping onto stony beaches through the drizzle. Mind you, leaving the front and rear windows and frames intact and wound up would have made these pretty civilised as convertible cars go.

Other companies developed even posher Minis to join the Wolseleys and Rileys. Radford and Wood & Pickett were coachbuilders whose market was evaporating as the demand for coachbuilt cars dwindled to nothing. The Silver Wraith was the last coachbuilt Rolls-Royce still supplied as a chassis delivered to a body constructor, and its production ended in 1959.

Radford absorbed another coachbuilder, Freestone & Webb, but the coachbuilding companies were really having to scratch around as the '60s progressed. When people like Ringo Starr with an endless supply of money wanted custom Minis, the surviving coachbuilders cheerfully obliged. Vanden Plas was another previously independent coachbuilding company, bought by BMC and reduced to a posh badge on BMC 1100s and 1300s and

moment as I'm chewing over an idea for a new book called *You Are What You Drive*, which will make some people feel smug, but will seriously upset others. It could be an actively dangerous book to write, but could also be top fun.

Within the rarefied world of BMC's posh Minis, there were subtle gradations. The Wolseley Hornet is just slightly downmarket from the Riley Elf, which you can tell by the smaller acreage of veneer on its dashboard.

Elves and Hornets shared a modified Mini bodyshell, with a little boot added that sported trendy fins, and bonnet and front panel modifications that incorporated a small version of the traditional Wolseley and Riley grille shells. Refinements such as air vents, wind-up windows and concealed door hinges appeared on Rileys and Wolseleys before showing up on ordinary pleb Minis. Around 30,000 of each model were made.

on an upmarket version of the Austin Westminster known as the Vanden Plas Princess 4-litre R, which was fitted with a Rolls-Royce engine and was originally to have been badged as a Bentley.

Radford in 1963 were selling three posh Mini variants – the Radford Mini de Ville, Bel Air and Deluxe models, variously loaded with goodies. Features included Benelite grilles with foglamps, padded and leather-trimmed seats, woolly carpets, Webasto sliding sunroofs, and so on. Instruments were multifarious, chrome-bezelled and set in walnut-veneered leather-bound pods. Headlamps came in for much custom work, as they are the 'eyes' of a car and can make a major styling statement. Lucas tripod P700 headlights in chrome cowls were a favourite, but there were also stacked double headlights and vertical oblong headlights sourced from Facel Vega. Facel was a seriously upmarket French car builder whose cars usually cost as much as several houses.

Radford's electric Mini windows were a novel and dramatic luxury in the UK of the 1960s, and were of the same type used in Rolls-Royces: massive overkill electric motors with steel chains to haul the glass up and down. The doors of a Radford shut with a hefty thud, not with a click or a clonk. Radfords are also very nice to drive, having benefited from all the coachbuilders' noise-reduction tricks. They also weigh a good bit more, and that's part of the formula.

In 1965 Radford's hatchback Mini appeared, the Mini de Ville GT, with most of the rear-end bodywork welded into a single panel that hinged upwards. Peter Sellers ordered one for Britt Ekland.

Wood & Pickett's Margrave offered the same sort of conversions as Radford, using twin sideways headlights with their own small grille, or Mercedes vertical headlights. W&P finished up doing rather better commercially than Radford in the end, despite a tendency to make white leather interiors. Or perhaps because of it.

↓ I have no idea why it required an independent coachbuilder to take the obvious step of changing the Mini into a far more useful hatchback, rather than the car's manufacturer.

↑→ Ogle Design produced a sharp and sexy body on the Mini floorpan, completely obscuring its origin but not its performance and handling. Although proportionally similar to a Mini Marcos, it's as stylistically cohesive as the Marcos isn't.

ERA Minis, converted by English Racing Automobiles in the late 1980s, retained the Mini bodyshell but stuffed in an MG Metro Turbo engine. Modifications included bodyshell changes to the arches to fit 13in wheels, and to the bulkhead to make room for the turbocharger, as well as a reverse scoop at the back of the bonnet to reduce engine bay temperatures, extra water cooling and an oil cooler, and ECU changes. Their interiors featured much leather and instrumentation. Around 480 were built, most of them going to Japan.

The Ogle Mini was a more radical approach to posh Minis, with its own GRP bodywork mounted on the Mini floorpan. It was produced from 1960 through to 1963/4. Sixty-six were built, of which 26 have apparently survived. The Ogle was built from a new Mini Cooper, which was cut down to a floorpan, reinforced, rustproofed and used as a base for a very pretty GRP bodyshell. It was supplied complete rather than as a kit, although it's available in kit form now. Mechanicals remained Mini, although the interior was more like a Mini Marcos with bucket seats, wood dash and steering wheel, and a sports-car rather than shopping-car collection of instruments. Ogle Design was also responsible for the original elegant and stylish Reliant Scimitar, originally intended to be a Daimler. They also styled the Reliant Robin, but let's not rub that in.

New Ogle Minis can now be bought from NostalgiaCars.co.uk. These are entirely approved by Ogle Design and bear continuation chassis numbers: they're unchanged from the early '60s originals apart from better seat belt mountings and rustproofing.

A new idea that has just popped up as a result of writing this chapter is to create a Mini that never was. My own Mini, featured now and again in the Logbook section of *MiniWorld*, is known as Bubble because it is champagne-coloured and also because of some rust bubbles under the paint, which are gradually achieving increased prominence as time goes on. Bubble is a 1978 Canadian Mini 1000, and apart from amusing/grotesque Canada-only impact bumpers, it is not a very exciting Mini as Minis go: the 1978 interior in particular is semi-modernised, plasticky and cheap, so any change would be an improvement.

The MG Mini is the major tooth missing in the Mini's lifetime grin. There were Riley Minis and Wolseley Minis, but there was never an MG Mini. The Morris/Austin 1100/1300 was sold in Riley Kestrel and Wolseley 1100 versions, and there was also an MG 1100/1300, which would offer some guidance as to what the specifications of an MG Mini might have been.

Two options present themselves. The MG Mini might have, or ought to have, happened concurrently with the

Rileys and Wolseleys in the 1960s, so in that case Bubble would get a 1275 with two SUs, disc brakes, possibly hydrolastic suspension, and a bonnet and front panel shape shared with Elves and Hornets but with a slightly different MG grille. I could fabricate that from an adapted MGA grille, cut down to Elf/Hornet size and rechromed. Whether the back end should be extended in Elf/Hornet style or not is debatable. There was a bumless Wolseley variant with a normal Mini rear end sold in South Africa, so the precedent is there.

Seating could be either leather or vinyl, and the dash would definitely need some woodwork and a tacho at the very least. There would be chrome or stainless body trim aplenty, much MG badgery everywhere, and two-tone paint – 'Varitone' paint jobs are an MG tradition.

The other option is an imaginary MG Mini Turbo from the 1980s, which would have been achieved by filleting all the good bits out of an MG Metro Turbo and jamming them into a Mini shell. I don't really understand why the company didn't go for either MG Mini option: but then I also don't understand why they stopped developing MGBs, Midgets and Triumph Spitfires and handed that whole market segment, gift-wrapped, to Mazda. Perhaps all the incompetent managers who were promoted out of the way finally made it to the top.

As well as the missing MG Mini, there is also no Vanden Plas Mini, although the Vanden Plas 1100/1300 is a close cousin. As to whether a Vanden Plas Mini would have been more or less posh than a Radford or a Wood & Pickett, that is a matter for future saloon-bar debate. Although to kick off the debate, it has to be said that tailored cars are a lot posher than even the most upmarket off-the-shelf ones.

More mad Minis

I'm still the North American correspondent for *MiniWorld*, and still coming across excellent Minis all the time. Here are a few more top cars for which we didn't have space earlier in the book to cover them in all their glory.

A few years ago, jamming a big Honda engine into a Mini and making a decent job of it was radical enough to guarantee a feature, but Mini builders have moved onwards and upwards, and have responded to the challenge: the Honda engine is just the starting point now, and more and mad Minis appear all the time. Mini Rules OK, and long may it reign.

↑ Just chopping the roof makes a Mini look fat and squat, but doing the job properly and cutting a slice out of the main bodywork is a massive undertaking.

→ The body is cut quite a long way down – you can see that the lights sit low and the whole bodyshell is lowered compared to the wheels. The car still runs 10-inch wheels and tyres.

Sprint replica

Kenny Benchek's sprint replica is chopped in the same way as the real thing – a chunk is taken out of the roof and also below the waistline. A serious bodywork challenge, many years in the making.

← The engine obviously sits a couple of inches higher in the lowered body, and Kenny had to remake the bonnet frame to allow enough clearance to shut the bonnet. The rocker cover and carb were also shaved.

↑ The lowered roof could make the interior claustrophobic if it weren't for the white Webasto slide-back sunroof.

Posh Riley Elf

At first glance Phil Taggart's Elf just looks nice and shiny. A closer look reveals just how nice, and a chat further reveals that twenty thousand dollars went into making it look this good. It also drives very nicely indeed, and is seriously comfy with its Hydrolastic suspension and fresh ostrich-pattern leather seats.

↑ Ostrich-patterned leather interior could be considered slightly over the top… but if it's good enough for a Bugatti, it's good enough for a Mini.

→ Phil's car looks way better than it did when it was new. It may have been the poshest of the standard Minis, but it never gleamed as it does now.

↓ The chrome-plating bill must have taken quite a chunk of the fat restoration cost: it's up to show standards.

Monster 4x4

This looks quite harmless, but the grey primer finish is because this car is still a prototype. BJ and Norman at Minitec in Georgia can't leave well alone, and after developing a DIY Honda conversion kit for Minis, they dismantled a Honda 4x4 CR-V shopping jeep and got the entire 4x4 drivetrain out of it. Their rear-Honda-engine kit is currently in development too… check out www.superfastminis.com

⬇ It just looks a bit naughty at a glance, but those wheels are suspiciously big, and isn't the front end longer than it ought to be?

◣ Here's why. Stonking Vtec Honda engine, and six times the original power. With all four wheels gripping and a ridiculous power-to-weight ratio, this has to be a major hoot to drive.

⬇ The cabin looks a bit sparse, but the shell and floor is still mostly Mini, although gear lever and pedals are custom. Box for feet is interesting: there must be issues with room under the toeboard, or perhaps it was built with Nicolas Sarkozy in mind.